FINANCIAL INSTRUMENTS

Complete Guide to Stocks, Bonds, other Equity & Debt Instruments

+ Derivatives, Money Markets, ETFs, Funds, Valuation, Regulation, Market Analysis, Taxes, and Advanced Trading Techniques

STEPHEN EXAFIN-WELLINGTON

www.exafin.net

INTRODUCTION

Welcome to the new Guide to Financial Instruments from EXAFIN! You may be a novice investor, a student, or a seasoned professional seeking a refresher—whatever your stance... This new resource of ours is your structured path through the complexity of the various financial tools, offering clarity and in-depth insight into fundamental aspects of financial markets. Let's see an overview of what we will explore!

1. FOUNDATIONAL CONCEPTS
Understanding what financial instruments are, identifying their varied types, and acknowledging the inherent risk-reward trade-offs, are imperative first steps in your exploration of financial markets.

2. EQUITY INSTRUMENTS
From understanding the basics of *common* and *preferred stocks* to exploring the dynamics of *stock exchanges, IPOs, ETFs,* and other equity instruments, this section unveils the core concepts of ownership in companies.

3. DEBT INSTRUMENTS
Dive into the realm of debt, deciphering the nature and applications of instruments like *bonds, CDs,* and *mortgage-backed securities,* and understanding the nuances of lending to corporations and governments.

4. DERIVATIVES
These instruments offer a complex but rewarding facet of finance: understand the intricacies of *futures contracts, options, swaps,* and delve into the world of *exotic derivatives.*

5. MONEY MARKETS

Discover the operations and instruments of *money markets,* understanding the role of *Treasury Bills, Repos,* and money market funds in short-term financing.

6. RISK MANAGEMENT

Risk is intrinsic to finance: learn about strategies such as *hedging,* and acquaint yourself with the methods of *risk assessment* and the importance of *credit ratings.*

7. VALUATION

From Discounted Cash Flows (*DCF*) to *option pricing* models, explore how financial instruments are valued and understand the methodologies employed in the process.

8. REGULATION AND COMPLIANCE

Ensure your financial knowledge adheres to regulatory compliance by understanding the role and regulations imposed by bodies like the SEC and FINRA.

9. MARKET ANALYSIS

Market analysis is pivotal to informed investment. Dive into *technical* and *fundamental analysis,* and explore the role psychology plays in financial markets through *behavioral finance.*

10. TAXES AND FINANCIAL INSTRUMENTS

Navigate through the tax implications pertaining to financial instruments, understanding the nuances of *capital gains, losses,* and how *dividends* and *interest income* are taxed.

11. ETHICAL CONSIDERATIONS

Acknowledge the importance of ethics in finance, exploring facets of socially responsible investing and legalities concerning insider trading and market manipulation.

12. ADVANCED TOPICS

Delve into complex areas of finance such as *algorithmic* and *high-frequency trading* and explore the esoteric worlds of *dark pools* and *private exchanges.*

➔ This guide is structured to **gradually build your understanding** from foundational concepts to advanced topics, assuring a coherent and comprehensive comprehension of financial instruments and markets. Whether you peruse from cover to cover or seek insights into specific topics, may this guide serve as a valuable resource in your financial exploration and decision-making journey.

In the hope that you find this work illuminating, have a good journey through its contents!

1. FOUNDATIONAL CONCEPTS

1.1 What Are Financial Instruments?

Financial instruments are the building blocks of the entire financial system. No exaggeration, no fluff. Understand what they are, and you've got the key to understanding how money flows, how wealth is created, and yes, sometimes lost.

So, what exactly are financial instruments? In plain English, a financial instrument is a contract. That's right, a piece of paper—or these days, more likely a digital record—that represents a financial relationship between parties. This is the magic wand that turns your money into assets or liabilities, depending on which side of the fence you're standing.

Think about it. You buy a stock? That's a financial instrument. You take out a mortgage? Yep, that's another one. What about your college loans, your retirement funds, even the money market account where you stashed some emergency cash? All financial instruments. See, you're already deeper in this world than you thought, and knowing how to navigate it can be the difference between living paycheck-to-paycheck and achieving financial freedom.

You might be wondering, "Why the heck do we need so many types of these things?" Great question. Life is complicated, and so are financial needs. Imagine trying to build a skyscraper using only a hammer and nails. Impossible, right? Just like that, you can't have a complex, modern financial system with only one type of financial instrument. You need variety for different needs: short-term, long-term, high-risk, low-risk, and everything in between.

At its core, a financial instrument is designed to move money from people who have it to those who need it. You've got extra cash? Buy a bond, and you're lending your money to a corporation or government. You need to hedge against inflation? Purchase some commodity futures. Simple as that.

But here's the catch: All this movement of money comes with risks and rewards, and this is why you can't just wade into this like a toddler at a swimming pool. There's the potential for profit, sure, but also for loss—sometimes colossal loss if you don't know what you're doing. That's why we have whole sectors of the economy, and armies of analysts and experts, dedicated to understanding these instruments.

So, you might be asking, "How do I know which financial instrument is right for me?" Sit tight. This book is going to lay it all out, from the bread-and-butter stuff like stocks and bonds to the spicier fare like derivatives and exotic options. You'll learn not just what they are, but how to use them to your advantage.

It's like learning the rules of the road before you get behind the wheel of a car. You need to know what a stop sign means, how to navigate a roundabout, and what those road lines signify. In the same vein, mastering financial instruments is a must before you get on the financial highway. Not knowing could lead to some serious financial fender-benders.

To wrap this up, get this ingrained in your mind: financial instruments are not just Wall Street jargon. They're real, they're everywhere, and they dictate how money flows in our lives and our world. Understanding them is not optional; it's necessary.

Because once you do, you're no longer just a passenger in your financial journey—you're in the driver's seat.

This isn't just theory; it's practical knowledge that's going to empower you to make informed decisions. So stick around. We're just getting started, and trust me, you won't look at your wallet or your bank account the same way ever again.

1.2 Types of Financial Instruments: Equity, Debt, Derivatives

The financial market is a vast jungle, and these instruments are the wildlife. More specifically, they fall into three big categories: Equity, Debt, and Derivatives. Get to know these, and you'll navigate the jungle like a pro.

Equity Instruments
Let's kick it off with equity. Think ownership. Think piece of the pie. When you buy an equity instrument, such as common or preferred stock, you're buying a piece of a company. This isn't just a transaction; it's a relationship. You are now a shareholder. Welcome to the club. When the company profits, so do you—through dividends or a rising stock price. But beware, if the company stumbles, your investment can take a hit.

Debt Instruments
Next up, debt instruments. In simplest terms, you're the lender, and someone else is the borrower. You're not owning; you're loaning. Bonds, certificates of deposit, and commercial paper fall under this category. You lend your money, and in return, you get a promise to be paid back with interest. Sounds simple, but remember, not all borrowers are created equal. Some are riskier than others, and that risk is usually offset by higher interest rates.

Derivatives
Now, for the third wheel—derivatives. These are the chameleons of the financial world. They derive their value from other financial instruments like stocks, bonds, or commodities. Think of them as

bets on future price movements. Futures, options, and swaps are your main culprits here. You're not buying an asset; you're entering a contract to buy or sell an asset at a future date at a predetermined price. This is high-stakes, high-reward territory. With the right moves, you can make a killing, but get it wrong, and you can lose your shirt.

Here's where it gets juicy. Each of these types has its own subcategories and variations. For instance, with equity, you can go traditional with common stocks or opt for something more nuanced like preferred stocks or even something more complex like real estate investment trusts (REITs). Each comes with its own set of rules, and you need to understand them if you're going to play the game and win.

Debt is not just about lending money and getting it back with interest. There are flavors to this. You can go the safer route with government bonds, or maybe you like a little spice and opt for junk bonds, which carry higher risks but also higher returns. The point is, it's not one-size-fits-all. You've got options, and those options are your tools.

Derivatives are where the pros play. These are not for the faint-hearted. They can offer enormous leverage, meaning you can control a large asset for a fraction of its price. But remember, with great power comes great responsibility—or in this case, great risk. Derivatives can make you rich quick, but they can also flatten you in no time if you don't know what you're doing.

Now, listen closely. This is critical. Each type of financial instrument carries its own risk profile. Don't just dive in without knowing how deep the water is. Equity is generally considered riskier than debt, but with potentially higher returns. Debt is considered safer, but the returns are usually lower. Derivatives? They're the wild cards—extremely volatile but potentially extremely profitable.

Remember, the point is not to fear these different types of financial instruments but to understand them. Each has its place, and each serves a specific function in your financial arsenal. Used correctly, they can provide not just returns, but also diversification and a hedge against risks.

You're not going to be an expert overnight, but that's fine. Even the sharpest Wall Street minds had to start somewhere. What matters is you're now in the game. But unlike a casino, this isn't about luck. It's about skill, knowledge, and strategy.

➔ So there you have it. Equity, Debt, and Derivatives. These are your main building blocks, your primary colors. Mix them right, and you could paint yourself a financial masterpiece. Get it wrong, and you'll end up with financial mud. But don't worry. Stick with me, and we'll turn you into a financial Picasso in no time.

1.3 Risk and Reward: The Fundamental Trade-Off

Risk and Reward, the Yin and Yang of the financial world. No fluff, no filler—just the unvarnished truth. You need to understand this concept inside and out because it's the axis around which the financial world spins.

Risk: The Cost of Doing Business

First off, let's talk about risk. It's the 800-pound gorilla in the room, and it's not going away, so you might as well get to know it. Risk is the probability of losing your hard-earned cash. It's the fine print, the "terms and conditions" of the financial world. Whenever you invest in anything—stocks, bonds, derivatives—you're taking on risk. It's the cost of doing business in the world of finance.

Think of it as the flip side of opportunity. The possibility of loss is the price you pay for the chance to make money. No risk, no reward. It's as simple as that.

There are many types of risk: market risk, credit risk, operational risk—the list goes on. And the thing about risk is that it's sneaky. It's often not where you expect it to be. That's why diversification—spreading your investments across different types of assets—is so crucial. The idea is to not put all your eggs in one basket, lest the basket falls and you're left with a mess.

Reward: The Light at the End of the Tunnel

On to the happier topic: reward. This is the reason we all show up to the investing party. It's the return on investment (ROI), the profit, the gains—the sweet nectar of financial success. Just as there are multiple forms of risk, there are different types of rewards. It can be a dividend payment from a stock you own, interest from a bond, or capital gains from selling an asset at a higher price than you paid for it.

Balancing Act

Now, here's the kicker: Risk and reward are two sides of the same coin. Want higher rewards? Be prepared to assume higher risks. It's a dance, a balancing act. You can't have one without the other. Take the stock market, for example. When you invest in stocks, you're looking for capital gains. But guess what? Stocks are volatile; they can shoot up, but they can also crash and burn. You take on that volatility—that risk—in hopes of a big payoff.

On the other hand, suppose you prefer a safer bet like government bonds. The risk is low, but so is the reward. You can't expect to make a killing with a low-risk asset. The trade-off is always there, lurking in the background.

The Utility of Risk Assessment

You might wonder, how do you quantify risk? It sounds like an elusive creature. Well, it's not. Financial markets have come up with all sorts of metrics and models to quantify risk. The Sharpe ratio, Beta, standard deviation—these are not just jargon. They are tools you can use to measure the risk associated with different investments. And once you can measure risk, you can manage it.

Risk Tolerance: Know Thyself

Before you go diving into the financial markets, take a hard look in the mirror. What's your risk tolerance? Are you the thrill-seeking type who lives for volatility, or does the mere thought of losing money keep you up at night? Be honest with yourself. Because here's another truth bomb: Your psychological comfort is as crucial as any financial metric. Investing in something that's too risky for your taste can lead to poor decision-making and, ultimately, to financial loss.

The Irrefutable Law of Risk and Reward

The fundamental law of risk and reward is irrefutable. You cannot escape it, but you can navigate it with intelligence and strategy. Your job as an investor is not to eliminate risk—that's impossible—but to optimize it. That means finding the sweet spot where the potential reward justifies the risk you're taking.

➔ To recap: risk is unavoidable, but it's not a villain. It's merely the price of admission to the financial playground. Reward is what you're after, but it doesn't come free. The two are eternally linked in a dance that you, as an investor, must learn to navigate. No shortcuts, no cheat codes, just a fundamental truth that you'll do well to remember: the trade-off between risk and reward is the linchpin of your financial life. Get it right, and the possibilities are limitless. Get it wrong, and you're setting yourself up for a world of pain. Choose wisely.

2. EQUITY INSTRUMENTS

2.1 Common Stock: Ownership in a Company

Let's dive right into the deep end of the pool: we're talking about Common Stock, the bread and butter of equity investing. This is not just a piece of paper or a digital entry on your brokerage account; it's your ticket to the ownership club of a company. No beating around the bush—when you buy common stock, you own a piece of the action. You're not a bystander; you're a participant. Let's break this down.

The Essence of Common Stock

You're buying a sliver, a tiny fraction, of a company when you purchase common stock. This is the real deal. You get a say in how the company is run—albeit a small one—and you get a piece of the profits, commonly known as dividends. You also have the potential to make money by selling your shares at a higher price than what you paid for them. That's capital gains, my friend.

The Voting Power

Common stock usually comes with voting rights. These rights allow you to have a say in corporate matters, like who gets to sit on the board of directors. Let's be clear; your voice is proportional to the number of shares you own. If you own a single share out of a billion, don't expect the CEO to call you for advice. But hey, it's still a voice, and that's more than what debt investors get.

Dividends and Capital Gains

Now, what's in it for you? Two things: dividends and capital gains. Dividends are your cut of the company's profits, usually paid out quarterly. But remember, not all companies pay dividends. Some prefer to reinvest all their profits for growth. As for capital gains, that's the money you make when you sell your stock for more than you bought it. Simple, right?

The Risk Factor

Don't get too comfortable. Owning common stock is risky. You're at the bottom of the totem pole when it comes to getting your money back if the company goes under. Bondholders, preferred stockholders—they all get paid before you do. So, yes, higher rewards come with higher risks. Get used to it.

Liquidity and Market Behavior

One of the beauties of common stock is liquidity. You can buy or sell it almost instantaneously during market hours. But be warned, the stock market is a volatile beast. Prices fluctuate based on a ton of factors—earnings reports, geopolitical events, market sentiment—and sometimes for no discernable reason at all.

The Power of Research

Before you even think about clicking that "buy" button, do your homework. Analyze the company's financials, scrutinize its management, evaluate its competitive position. You wouldn't buy a car without checking under the hood, would you? The same principle applies here. Due diligence is not optional; it's mandatory.

Tax Implications

Let's not forget Uncle Sam. You'll have to pay taxes on any dividends you receive and on any capital gains you realize. The taxman always wants his cut.

The Golden Rule: Diversification

Never, and I mean NEVER, put all your money into a single stock. No matter how solid or promising it seems, diversification is your best friend. Spread your bets to mitigate the inherent risks of stock investing.

Summing It Up

Owning common stock is as real as it gets in the investment world. You're a part-owner of a business. You get to vote, you get a cut of the profits, and you get the potential for capital gains. But remember, with great power comes great responsibility—and risk. Do your due diligence, diversify your holdings, and keep an eye on tax implications.

➔ So... buying common stock is like entering into a high-stakes partnership. You're in it for the long haul, and you need to be vigilant, educated, and ever so slightly daring. So go ahead, take the plunge—but make sure you know the depth of the waters you're diving into. That's the crux of what common stock is all about. No sugarcoating, no fluff, just the straight-up, unvarnished truth. Happy investing!

2.3 Stock Exchanges and Over-The-Counter Markets

You want to buy or sell stocks? You need a venue, a marketplace. That's where stock exchanges and over-the-counter (OTC) markets come into play. Think of them as the eBay and Craigslist for your stocks. One is more formal with plenty of rules, and the other is like the Wild West of financial markets.

Stock Exchanges: The Wall Street Glamour

When people think of stock trading, they often visualize Wall Street, ticker tapes, and frenzied floor traders. That's the stock exchange for you, the most formal platform for buying and selling equities. Think NYSE, NASDAQ, London Stock Exchange—these are the celebrity venues of finance. They offer a regulated, transparent environment to transact. You want to be part of the big league? This is where you belong.

What's So Great About It?

Three words: Liquidity, Transparency, and Regulation. These exchanges are packed with action. Stocks are being bought and sold at every tick of the clock. You want to sell 1,000 shares of Apple? Boom, done. You get real-time price discovery, which means you always know the current price of the stock you're eyeing.

And let's talk about oversight. These exchanges are like Fort Knox when it comes to rules and regulations. Think of the Securities and Exchange Commission (SEC) as the ever-watchful guardian, ensuring you're not getting scammed.

Over-The-Counter Markets: The Back Alleys of Finance

Now, let's switch gears and head to the less glitzy, but incredibly versatile world of OTC markets. No centralized floor, no opening bell, just a network of dealers connected electronically. Here you'll find the stocks that are not big or glamorous enough to make it to the major exchanges. But don't dismiss them; there's gold to be found here.

Why Should You Care?

Freedom and Variety. OTC markets are like the expansive countryside compared to the gated community of stock exchanges. You'll find not just equities, but derivatives, currencies, and more. Penny stocks? They're here. Bonds? Right this way. Foreign stocks that haven't touched U.S soil? Welcome aboard.

But beware, with freedom comes responsibility. There's less regulation, which means due diligence is on you, buddy. Prices aren't as transparent, and you might not find a buyer or seller as quickly as on an exchange.

The Hybrid Creatures: ECNs and ATS

Here's the twist. We have platforms that are neither purely stock exchanges nor solely OTC markets. Meet Electronic Communication Networks (ECNs) and Alternative Trading Systems (ATS). They act as mini-exchanges, matching buyers with sellers electronically. They offer some of the transparency of exchanges but operate in the flexible landscape of OTC markets.

Let's Talk About Listing

Stocks don't just appear on exchanges. They get listed, often through an IPO or Direct Listing, another topic we'll dive into later. OTC stocks can also move up to an exchange if they meet specific criteria, like minimum market capitalization or share price. It's like graduating from community college to an Ivy League university.

Arbitrage Opportunities

Pay attention to this: Stocks sometimes get listed on multiple exchanges or even on an exchange and an OTC market. Savvy traders exploit the tiny price differences between these platforms for risk-free profits. Yeah, you heard it right, risk-free, if done correctly.

Transaction Costs

Last but not least, costs. Stock exchanges often have higher transaction costs, what with all their rules and infrastructure. OTC trading could be cheaper, but remember, cheaper isn't always better, especially if you're sacrificing transparency and liquidity.

Bottom Line

Stock exchanges and OTC markets serve the same essential function: they facilitate the buying and selling of financial instruments. However, they are as different as night and day in their operations, level of oversight, and even the kinds of assets you can trade. Understanding these differences isn't just academic; it's fundamental to knowing where and how you want to trade.

➔ So there you have it, the battlefield and the bazaar of financial trading. Choose your playground wisely, and always know the rules of the game. Next!

2.4 IPOs and Direct Listings

Companies don't just magically appear on stock exchanges. No, sir. There's a grand debut, a sort of financial coming-of-age ceremony, where companies go from privately-held to publicly-traded. This transformation happens through two main avenues: Initial Public Offerings (IPOs) and Direct Listings. Grab your seat; the show's about to start.

Initial Public Offerings (IPOs): The Red Carpet Affair
Picture this: A company decides it wants to go public. Why? More money, more growth, and sometimes, just the allure of ringing that opening bell at the NYSE or NASDAQ. Now, here comes the red carpet, the glam, the whole shebang. That's an IPO for you.

How Does It Work?
You've got investment bankers, underwriters, analysts—basically, the crème de la crème of finance—helping the company price and issue new shares to the public. The bankers drum up investor interest with a roadshow, and based on demand, they price the shares. The public gets a first chance to buy, and the company gets a nice cash influx. Sounds terrific, right?

The Catch
Ah, but not so fast. You see, IPOs are expensive, complicated, and time-consuming. Investment bankers don't come cheap, and they usually get a chunky percentage of the funds raised. Regulatory requirements? A laundry list of them. Audits, prospectuses, SEC filings—you name it. Plus, early investors and insiders often have to sit tight due to lock-up periods, during which they can't sell their shares.

Direct Listings: The No-Frills Path

Now, imagine a company that doesn't need the glitz and glam, just a straightforward entry into the public market. Enter Direct Listings.

How Does It Work?

In a Direct Listing, no new shares are created. Existing shareholders, think employees and early investors, directly sell their shares to the public. No investment bankers setting the price, no underwriters buying up shares, just a pure, unadulterated market mechanism at work.

The Catch

Sounds liberating, but here's the kicker: no guaranteed funds for the company. In IPOs, investment banks often buy unsold shares. In Direct Listings, you're leaving things to market dynamics. If there's no demand, tough luck. And let's not forget, without the promotional roadshow, a Direct Listing can go unnoticed, lost in the cacophony of the financial markets.

The Criteria: Who Chooses What?

For young companies starved for capital, IPOs are generally the way to go. For well-established companies with enough cash in the coffers—think Spotify or Palantir—a Direct Listing makes more sense. You skip the underwriter fees, avoid diluting ownership, and still get your ticker symbol flashing on trading screens worldwide.

The Financial Gymnastics

Both IPOs and Direct Listings require a ton of preparation. You're not just tossing your company into the stock market abyss; you're performing financial gymnastics. Financial statements need to be scrubbed cleaner than a surgical suite. Corporate governance?

Needs to be tighter than Fort Knox. Transparency isn't optional; it's mandated by law.

Picking a Side

There's no universally right or wrong choice here, just the one that fits your company's needs. IPOs offer the glamour and capital but come with costs and complications. Direct Listings offer speed and simplicity but lack the guaranteed capital injection.

Bottom Line

IPO or Direct Listing—it's a choice companies make based on their financial health, needs, and goals. As an investor or market observer, knowing the difference isn't just trivia; it's key to understanding why a stock is entering the market the way it is, and what risks and rewards lie in store. Make no mistake; this isn't just another financial term in the jargon jungle. It's fundamental to the lifecycle of companies and, by extension, the dynamics of the capital markets.

➔ So, there it is—your no-nonsense guide to IPOs and Direct Listings. Trust me, this is information you'll want in your financial toolkit. Got it? Good. On to the next.

2.5 ETFs and Mutual Funds

Let's get to the heart of the matter: Not everyone has the time, energy, or even the know-how to pore over financial reports, scrutinize balance sheets, or track individual stocks. And honestly, you don't have to. Enter ETFs and Mutual Funds—your ready-made investment portfolios in a box. These financial instruments are like those assorted boxes of chocolates—each piece is a different investment, and collectively, they provide a well-rounded treat for investors. So what makes these two different? Let's crack it open.

Exchange-Traded Funds (ETFs): The Flexible Innovators

ETFs are essentially investment funds that trade like a stock. You can buy and sell shares of an ETF throughout the day, just like you would with Apple or Tesla. Sounds neat, right?

How Does It Work?

An ETF holds a basket of stocks, bonds, or other assets. The idea is to replicate the performance of an underlying index like the S&P 500, or a specific sector, say, technology. What you get is instant diversification. One share of an ETF gives you tiny slices of multiple companies or assets. This way, if one falls flat on its face, you're not going down with it.

The Perks

ETFs come with a list of pros: low fees, tax-efficiency, and insane flexibility. You can buy or sell anytime during trading hours, short-sell them, or even use options. And because they aim to mimic an index or sector, they typically have lower fees than their more hands-on counterparts, Mutual Funds. Plus, ETFs allow for tax-loss harvesting, a nifty feature for tax management.

Mutual Funds: The Tried-and-True

Before ETFs took the stage, Mutual Funds were the go-to option for pooled investments. Managed by professional portfolio managers, Mutual Funds are all about active investment. They're not just mirroring an index; they're trying to beat it.

How Does It Work?

A Mutual Fund pools money from multiple investors to buy a diversified portfolio of stocks, bonds, or other securities. You buy shares directly from the fund, usually at the end-of-day net asset value (NAV), not on the open market. A pro team of analysts and portfolio managers do the heavy lifting, picking investments they believe will outperform.

The Perks

First, you're leveraging professional expertise. These managers live and breathe finance; they're the special forces of investment. Mutual Funds can also delve into more complex investment strategies that ETFs typically avoid. Plus, they offer more investment styles and themes, catering to a wider range of investor needs and goals.

The Trade-offs

While Mutual Funds offer active management, they often come with higher fees—known as expense ratios—and potential load charges, which are commissions paid when buying or selling the fund. And let's be real: not all Mutual Funds beat the market, despite charging for the effort. In contrast, ETFs usually have lower fees but don't promise the moon—they aim to match the market, not beat it.

Making Your Pick

Both instruments offer diversification, but your choice boils down to your investment style and needs. Do you want day-to-day trading and lower costs? ETFs are your game. Do you prefer the idea of professionals making choices for you, even if it means higher fees? Mutual Funds could be your lane.

Why This Matters

You can't—and shouldn't—put all your eggs in one basket. Both ETFs and Mutual Funds provide a way to invest in a variety of assets without the headache of individual selection. They're cornerstones of a balanced investment strategy, serving both novice investors and Wall Street veterans.

➔ So... ETFs and Mutual Funds are like investment buffets, each with its unique flavor and cost. They're more than just footnotes in the investment world; they're the backbone of diversified portfolios. They represent democracy in investing, making it accessible and manageable for just about anyone interested in growing their money. Don't skim over these investment vehicles. Understand them. Choose wisely. And most importantly, use them as tools to build a more robust, more resilient financial future. Now, go ahead and pick your investment buffet.

2.6 Stock Options and Warrants

Stop for a moment and think about leverage—the art of getting more with less. In the realm of equity instruments, nothing embodies the spirit of leverage quite like Stock Options and Warrants. These are not just tickets to potential ownership; they're tickets with special privileges. Now, let's cut through the fog and really understand these two vehicles.

Stock Options: The Insider's Passport
A Stock Option is an agreement that gives you the right, but not the obligation, to buy or sell a stock at a predetermined price within a specific time frame. Simply put, it's like placing a small bet on a big game, and you get to decide whether to call it off.

How Does It Work?
In an options contract, you deal with two main types: call options and put options. A call option gives you the right to buy shares at a fixed price. A put option gives you the right to sell shares at a fixed price. The fixed price is called the "strike price," and the expiration date is when your option expires. Simple as that.

The Perks
Options are versatile tools. You can use them for hedging, to mitigate risks. Or you can go the speculative route and bet on stock price movements without owning the actual stock. The leverage is incredible—you control a large number of shares with a relatively small amount of money.

Warrants: The Outsider's Opportunity
Warrants are similar to options in many ways but come with their own unique characteristics. They are often issued by the company

itself, usually in conjunction with a bond or preferred stock issuance, to sweeten the deal and make the investment more attractive.

How Does It Work?

Like an option, a warrant gives you the right to buy shares of the company at a fixed price before expiration. However, when you exercise a warrant, the company issues new shares, unlike options, where no new shares are created. That's a key difference.

The Perks

The longevity of warrants is something to note. While options typically expire within weeks to a few years, warrants can last for several years, giving you a longer runway to exercise them. Also, because they often come bundled with other securities, they can offer a two-for-one kind of deal that could pay off handsomely.

The Trade-offs

Stock options can be complicated. Their values are influenced by various factors like volatility, time decay, and dividends. Plus, they require active management. If you're not careful, you can lose 100% of your investment in the blink of an eye. As for warrants, the main downside is dilution. When you exercise a warrant, you're adding to the total number of outstanding shares, which could dilute the share value.

Making Your Choice

Stock options are the tools of choice if you want flexibility and short-term strategies. They're ideal for hedging or making quick but calculated bets. Warrants, on the other hand, are for the long game and are often seen as bonus perks when buying other securities.

Why This Matters
Stock Options and Warrants are not just for Wall Street insiders or financial wizards. Understanding these instruments can level up your investment game. Whether you're an active trader looking to hedge your bets or a long-term investor eyeing a potentially lucrative side deal, these vehicles offer opportunities you don't want to ignore.

Let's not mince words: Options and warrants can be game-changers. They are financial instruments that offer massive leverage but come with their own sets of risks and rewards. If used wisely, they can supercharge your investment portfolio. But be wary; they are double-edged swords. Know them, understand the risks, and use them judiciously.

➔ Don't overlook stock options and warrants as elitist financial tools out of your reach. They're more accessible than you think and can be part of a diversified, strategic investment approach. So the next time someone mentions options or warrants, you'll know you're not just talking about simple stocks—you're talking about leverage, strategy, and a more sophisticated way to engage with the market.

3. DEBT INSTRUMENTS

3.1 Bonds: Lending to Corporations and Governments

Bonds: the word alone might evoke images of conservative investors or perhaps your grandparents talking about "safe" investments. Well, forget what you think you know about bonds, because they are neither boring nor the exclusive territory of risk-averse individuals. Bonds are, in fact, loans—loans that you provide either to a corporation or to a government. It's time to pull back the curtain on this powerhouse of an investment avenue.

What Are Bonds?

Simply put, a bond is a debt security. You're lending your money to an institution, and in return, they're promising to pay you back with interest. It's like becoming the bank for a short while. Unlike stocks, where you own a piece of the company, bonds make you a creditor. There are various types of bonds—corporate bonds, municipal bonds, and treasury bonds to name a few. But the basic principle remains the same: you lend money, you earn interest, and you get your principal back at the end of the term.

Why Bonds?

People adore bonds for their reliability. Let's be real: the stock market can be a rollercoaster. But bonds? They're the steady-Eddie income generators. In most cases, you know exactly what you're going to get and when you're going to get it. Interest payments arrive like clockwork and then—barring default—you get your original investment back.

How They Work

Here's the game: When a corporation or government needs capital, they issue bonds. These bonds have a 'face value'—usually in denominations like $1,000 or $5,000. They also come with a stated 'interest rate' and a 'maturity date.' You buy the bond at its face value. Every year, you collect the interest (known as a coupon). And when the bond reaches its maturity date, you get your initial investment back. The mechanics are as straightforward as lending your friend some money and charging interest.

TYPES OF BONDS

Corporate Bonds
Issued by companies to fund everything from operations to expansions. Corporate bonds generally offer higher interest rates because they come with more risk.

Government Bonds
Governments issue these to fund public projects. U.S. Treasury bonds are considered the gold standard of safety but offer lower yields.

Municipal Bonds
Local governments issue these to fund community projects. Often, the interest is tax-free, which can be a big advantage for investors.

The Risks
Let's not paint an overly rosy picture. Bonds are subject to risks like default, where the issuer can't pay back the principal or interest. Interest rate risk is another concern; if interest rates rise, the value of your existing bond drops. Inflation can also erode

your returns over time. However, compared to stocks, bonds are usually considered less risky.

Why This Matters

Bonds are an essential part of any well-rounded investment portfolio. They offer not only a buffer against the wild swings of the stock market but also a consistent income stream. And for those who do their homework, there are bonds to suit every risk appetite—from 'almost like cash' U.S. Treasuries to higher-yield corporate bonds that can offer stock-like returns.

The Bottom Line

The bond market is vast and varied, and it can be an excellent place to park your money for steady, if not spectacular, returns. Bonds offer a form of predictability that is hard to find in other financial instruments. They may not give you the adrenaline rush of watching a stock soar, but they offer financial stability and predictability that can be comforting, especially in volatile times.

➔ We have seen that bonds aren't just a "grandparent" investment. They are financial instruments with unique attributes that can serve multiple purposes, whether you're looking for regular income, safety, or a diversification tool. And remember, you're not just buying a piece of paper—you're essentially lending your money with the expectation of a return. So, the next time someone talks about bonds, know that you're discussing a cornerstone of financial markets and a pivotal part of any balanced investment portfolio.

3.2 Certificates of Deposit (CDs): The Uncelebrated Financial Haven

They're the quiet introverts at the financial instruments party—always present but often overlooked. But don't let their subdued nature fool you. Certificates of Deposit, in many respects, are the unsung heroes of the investment world. If you're seeking a stable, predictable, and, dare I say it, boring form of investment, then listen up. CDs are for you.

What Are Certificates of Deposit?

Let's strip away the jargon. A Certificate of Deposit is essentially a time deposit. You give your money to a bank, and they give you a certificate. This certificate binds you and the bank in a financial hug for a fixed period—could be as short as a few months or as long as several years. You can't touch your money during this time without facing penalties. But here's the kicker: in return, the bank pays you a fixed interest rate that is usually higher than what you'd earn in a savings account.

High Rates, Higher Rewards

Why bother with a CD? One word: Rates. In a world where interest rates are low enough to make even a snail look fast, CDs offer a way to lock in higher interest rates for a fixed period. It's like a savings account on steroids. You get a fixed return, and you know exactly when you'll get it.

THE DIFFERENT FLAVORS

Traditional CDs

The most basic form. Deposit your money, earn fixed interest, and withdraw it all after a predetermined period.

Variable-Rate CDs
These offer a variable interest rate tied to market changes. Riskier, but potentially more rewarding.

Jumbo CDs
For the big spenders, Jumbo CDs require a high minimum deposit but offer higher interest rates.

The Downside
Here's the crux. CDs are not for the impatient. Your money is essentially "locked up" for the period of the CD. If you withdraw early, you face penalties, which could eat into the interest you've earned. It's like entering into a pact with the bank: you shall not touch this money until the time is up.

Why This Investment Matters
In an era of volatile markets, geopolitical uncertainty, and social unrest, stability can be a very compelling feature. This is where CDs shine. They offer a predictable, low-risk return on your investment. That said, they're not for everyone. If you're young and have a high-risk tolerance, you may find CDs a bit stifling. But if you're approaching retirement or looking for a stable return for part of your portfolio, they're ideal.

Beyond the Personal
Certificates of Deposit don't just cater to individual investors. They're also a critical funding source for banks. When you open a CD, you're effectively lending money to the bank. The bank then uses these funds to provide loans or invest in other revenue-

generating activities. It's a symbiotic relationship: you get guaranteed returns, and the bank gets the liquidity it needs.

Quick Tips for CD Investors

1. *Shop Around*: Interest rates can vary significantly from one bank to another.
2. *Ladder Your CDs*: Don't put all your money into one long-term CD. Ladder them so that they mature at different times.
3. *Read the Fine Print*: Understand the penalties for early withdrawal.

➔ So we've seen how certificates of Deposit are an essential part of the financial ecosystem, both for individual investors seeking stability and for banks requiring liquidity. They're simple, straightforward, and a practical option for those looking for assured, albeit modest, returns. So, next time you're assessing your investment options, don't hastily pass over Certificates of Deposit. They might just be the uncelebrated financial haven you didn't know you needed. In the realm of financial instruments, they provide an important counterbalance to more volatile options, offering a reassuring blend of stability and guaranteed return. In a world full of financial unpredictability, the reliability of a CD can be a welcome respite.

3.3 Commercial Paper: The Unseen Backbone of Short-Term Finance

In the complex and multilayered universe of financial instruments, Commercial Paper may not catch your eye immediately. You might even miss it if you blink. But make no mistake—this unassuming financial tool is the lifeblood for countless corporations. A linchpin in the short-term financing landscape, Commercial Paper is both straightforward and instrumental.

What Is Commercial Paper?

Let's get to the point: Commercial Paper is an unsecured, short-term debt instrument issued by corporations to meet immediate financial needs like inventory purchase or payroll. Usually, it comes with a maturity period ranging from a few days to 270 days, and it's considered a highly liquid asset. Imagine it as an IOU on steroids, allowing corporations to get quick cash without the red tape usually associated with loans.

A Tool, Not a Toy

Commercial Paper is not child's play; it's a serious financial instrument primarily used by large, creditworthy corporations. That's because there's no collateral involved. Investors buy these papers based on the issuer's promise to return the money plus interest. If the issuer's creditworthiness is doubtful, the game is over before it even starts.

Why Do Companies Use It?

Time is money, and sometimes loans take too long. Commercial Paper enables companies to get immediate funds without the cumbersome procedures involved in traditional loans. This agility is often pivotal in the fast-paced world of business, allowing companies to seize opportunities or cover shortfalls promptly.

The Risk and Reward

Remember, Commercial Paper is unsecured. This means it carries higher risk compared to secured loans. But as compensation for the risk, it typically offers higher yields than government securities, making it attractive for investors seeking better short-term returns. However, be warned: if the issuing company defaults, you could lose your investment.

The Power of Ratings

Commercial Paper lives and dies by its credit rating. Agencies like Moody's and Standard & Poor's frequently rate these instruments. A high rating usually results in lower interest rates and vice versa. For investors, these ratings serve as a quick gauge for assessing the risk associated with a particular Commercial Paper.

TYPES OF COMMERCIAL PAPER

Asset-backed Commercial Paper

These are backed by other financial assets, usually receivables. They offer a tad more security but might come with slightly lower returns.

Tradeable Commercial Paper

These papers are usually listed on a stock exchange, offering greater liquidity but often at the cost of lower yields.

Bank Commercial Paper

Issued by banks, these are often considered less risky but may offer lower yields.

Regulatory Aspects

The U.S. commercial paper market is largely unregulated, but issuers must still adhere to the guidelines set by the Securities and Exchange Commission (SEC). Due to its short-term nature, Commercial Paper often escapes the rigorous scrutiny applied to other financial instruments, making it easier for corporations to issue them quickly.

A Multipurpose Tool

Commercial Paper isn't just for corporations. Many money market funds often invest in Commercial Paper to balance liquidity and yield. It's a versatile tool, serving a dual purpose of meeting corporate financing needs and providing investment options.

The Unseen Backbone

Why should you care? Because Commercial Paper plays a vital role in keeping the financial market wheels spinning. It serves as a quick, efficient funding source for companies and a lucrative short-term investment for money market funds, effectively tying different elements of the financial ecosystem together.

➔ Commercial Paper may not be the glitziest or most talked-about financial instrument, but its role is indispensable. It's the backstage crew that ensures the show goes on, making it possible for companies to operate smoothly and for investors to find attractive short-term options. Its simplicity and functionality make it a cornerstone in modern finance. So the next time you dive into the world of financial instruments, remember the unassuming yet pivotal role of Commercial Paper. In an arena filled with complexity, its straightforward effectiveness is a breath of fresh air.

3.4 Convertible Bonds: The Swiss Army Knife of Financial Instruments

If you've been exploring the maze-like world of financial instruments, you've probably encountered bonds and stocks, each with their own set of rules and peculiarities. But what if you're told there's a financial instrument that embodies the best of both worlds? Enter Convertible Bonds, the Swiss Army knife in your financial toolbox, versatile enough to adapt to changing market conditions.

What Are Convertible Bonds?

First things first, a Convertible Bond is a type of debt that can be converted into shares of the issuing company at a later date. It starts its life as a bond, earning interest for the investor. But it carries an embedded option to transform into equity shares at specific times and under certain conditions. It's like owning a hybrid car that can switch between gasoline and electricity, offering you flexibility and efficiency in one package.

Why Do Companies Issue Them?

Issuing Convertible Bonds is like throwing a curveball in a baseball game; it adds a level of complexity, but for a good reason. Companies do this to attract investors who might be wary of the risk associated with pure equity or pure debt. With Convertible Bonds, companies can offer the safety of a bond, while dangling the carrot of potential equity conversion, usually at a more favorable price than the current market rate.

The Power of Conversion

The most captivating feature of Convertible Bonds is the conversion aspect. When the company's stock price rises, the bondholder can convert the bonds into equity, reaping the benefits of stock appreciation. On the flip side, if the stock price tanks, the investor still gets regular interest payments, similar to a traditional bond.

The Price You Pay: Lower Yield

Nothing comes free in the world of finance. Convertible Bonds typically offer lower yields compared to regular bonds. This lower yield is the 'premium' you pay for the privilege of having the conversion option. It's a trade-off, like opting for a convertible car but sacrificing some fuel efficiency.

Hedging Your Bets

Think of Convertible Bonds as a hedging tool. If you're an investor sitting on the fence, unsure whether to back a promising but risky venture, Convertible Bonds offer a compromise. You get to support the company while mitigating downside risk through regular interest payments. And if the company thrives, your investment sprouts wings, converting into stock that could offer substantial gains.

Risks to Consider

Like any Swiss Army knife, Convertible Bonds are not without their risks. First, the issuer could default, though that risk exists for any bond. Second, you risk 'opportunity cost' because you're accepting lower yields compared to traditional bonds. Lastly, the conversion feature is often controlled by a set of complex rules defined by the issuer. Miss those fine-print details, and you might end up holding the short end of the stick.

Ratings and Regulations

Typically, Convertible Bonds are rated by credit rating agencies just like other bonds. Higher ratings indicate lower risk but also translate to lower yields. As for regulation, Convertible Bonds must adhere to the rules set by the SEC and other regulatory bodies, adding an extra layer of investor protection.

Real-world Uses

Convertible Bonds are often employed by high-growth companies, especially in sectors like technology and pharmaceuticals, where the potential for stock appreciation is significant. They are also popular in private equity deals, providing a secure yet flexible investment mechanism.

The Fine Print

Always read the terms and conditions. Conversion ratios, maturity dates, and other nitty-gritty details can significantly affect the bond's attractiveness. Make sure you fully understand these before investing.

➔ So... Convertible Bonds offer a unique blend of risk and reward, mixing elements from both the equity and debt realms. They may not be the easiest to understand, but their flexibility makes them one of the most intriguing financial instruments on the market. Whether you're a company looking for diversified funding or an investor seeking to hedge risks while retaining upside potential, Convertible Bonds are worth a close look. This Swiss Army knife may just be the versatile tool you need in your financial arsenal.

3.5 Mortgage-Backed Securities: The Double-Edged Sword of Financial Innovation

Mortgage-Backed Securities (MBS) are both genius and perilous, a financial innovation that can either propel economic growth or trigger devastating financial crises. By now, you've learned about straightforward financial instruments like bonds and stocks. Well, MBS are a bit more intricate; they are the Rubik's Cubes of the financial world.

What Exactly Are Mortgage-Backed Securities?

Imagine you're a bank that's given out a plethora of mortgages. You're sitting on a mountain of debt payments that'll trickle in over decades. Now, what if you could turn those slow-dripping future payments into immediate cash? This is where Mortgage-Backed Securities come into play. Essentially, banks bundle a group of mortgages together and then sell parts of that bundle to investors. These investors, in return, get periodic payments from the homeowners' mortgage payments.

Why Would Banks Do This?

At its core, the concept of MBS is about liquidity. Banks don't like waiting 30 years to get their money back; they want to lend more today. So, they sell off these mortgages to get quick cash, which can then be lent out again. The cycle repeats, money flows, and theoretically, everyone's happy—banks, new homeowners, and investors.

But Here's the Catch: Risk

Ah, yes, the eternal trade-off between risk and reward rears its head even here. If homeowners make their payments on time, everything runs like a well-oiled machine. But what if they don't? What if the economy tanks, people lose jobs, and those mortgage payments stop coming in? The MBS investors are left holding the bag. This isn't just theoretical; it was a massive domino that toppled during the 2008 financial crisis.

The Complexity Factor

Mortgage-Backed Securities can be as simple or as complex as a financial engineer wants them to be. Some MBS are sliced and diced into 'tranches,' each with different risk levels and yields. If this is starting to sound complicated, that's because it is. These complexities can obscure the true risks involved, lulling investors into a false sense of security.

Regulation: An Attempt at Safeguarding

After the 2008 debacle, regulators stepped in with various measures to make MBS less risky, or at least more transparent about their risks. However, regulation is always a game of catch-up. Financial innovation often outpaces the ability to fully understand and control it. So while regulation can mitigate some risks, it can't eliminate them entirely.

Investment Strategies

If you're considering investing in MBS, be warned: this is not a beginner's game. Understanding the nuances takes time and perhaps a strong stomach. However, the yield can be attractive, especially for those who can accurately price the risks involved.

Tax Considerations

Investing in MBS? Better keep the taxman in mind. Unlike traditional bonds, the tax implications of MBS can be more complex due to the return of principal amounts in each payment, rather than just at maturity. Consult a tax advisor if you're venturing into this territory.

The Ethical Dimension

Last but not least, there's an ethical layer to consider. The securitization of mortgages essentially turns basic human needs like housing into tradable commodities. This commodification can drive up home prices and exacerbate economic inequalities. It's a point worth pondering if you're contemplating dipping your toes into the MBS market.

➔ We've seen how on one hand, these securities are a brilliant financial innovation that enhances liquidity and can provide attractive investment opportunities. On the other hand, they're fraught with risks and complexities that can implode spectacularly if not managed well. If you decide to engage with MBS, do so with both eyes wide open, armed with a strong understanding of their intricacies and risks. They're not for everyone, but for those who master them, the rewards can be substantial. Just remember, handle with care.

4. DERIVATIVES

4.1 Futures Contracts: The Time Travelers of the Financial World

If the financial markets were a science fiction novel, futures contracts would be the time-traveling protagonists. They're the financial instruments that allow you to buy or sell an asset at a predetermined price at a specified time in the future. The concept is as mind-bendingly simple as it is revolutionary. You're essentially making a bet on the future, and like all forms of time travel, the journey is fraught with both opportunities and perils.

What Are Futures Contracts?

First things first—what exactly is a futures contract? It's an agreement between two parties to buy or sell an asset—be it commodities like oil, gold, or agricultural products, or financial assets like currency or stock indices—at a predetermined price at a specific date in the future. Unlike options, where the buyer has the option to exercise the contract, futures are obligatory. When the contract expires, the transaction must take place, whether you like it or not.

The Origin: Farmers and Commodities

Would you believe that futures contracts were born out of the need to hedge against the unpredictable nature of farming? Yep, that's right! Farmers wanted to lock in prices for their future harvests to safeguard against price fluctuations. It was essentially a risk management tool, and it still serves that purpose, although its applications have expanded astronomically.

Why Would You Use Futures?

Futures are used for both hedging and speculation. Hedging is for the cautious and the prudent; it's about reducing risk. If you're a company that needs to purchase raw materials regularly, you can use futures contracts to lock in prices, ensuring that even if market prices soar, your costs stay the same.

Speculation, on the other hand, is the playground of the daring. Traders use futures contracts to bet on price movements. If you think the price of oil will rise, you buy a futures contract. If the price does rise, you can sell the contract for a profit before it even expires.

The Leverage Factor
One of the most seductive—and dangerous—aspects of futures contracts is leverage. You can control a large asset for a fraction of its price. It's like buying a house with just the down payment, except in this case, even small market movements can yield significant profits—or losses.

The Zero-Sum Game
Futures are a zero-sum game. For every winner, there's a loser. When you profit, someone else incurs a loss. Unlike investing in stocks, where all parties can benefit from a company's growth, futures are more like a seesaw. It's thrilling, but remember, the stakes are high.

Taxes and Fees: The Hidden Costs
Dealing with futures? Make sure you read the fine print. Commissions, brokerage fees, and notably, tax implications, can nibble at your profits. Unlike long-term investments, futures are generally subject to short-term capital gains tax, which can be considerably higher.

The Unforgiving Complexity

Futures contracts can get complicated. They can be rolled over, meaning you can extend the contract into the future if you're not ready to settle it. There are also various types of orders, like stop orders and limit orders, designed to control how much you're willing to lose or gain. If you're not familiar with these terms, you'd better hit the books before diving in.

The Moral Quandary

Finally, let's touch on the ethical considerations. Futures trading, especially when it comes to commodities like food and energy, can impact real lives. If mass speculation drives up the price of wheat, for instance, it could lead to increased costs for consumers and even contribute to food shortages.

➔ **The Time Traveler's Dilemma**

Engaging with futures contracts is like stepping into a time machine. It offers the allure of foresight, the thrill of the gamble, and the security of hedging your bets. However, this financial time travel is not without its paradoxes and pitfalls. If you choose to journey down this road, do so with caution, adequate knowledge, and a clear understanding of the risks involved. Time travel, after all, is not for the faint of heart.

4.2 Options: Calls and Puts—The Chess Game of Finance

Options trading is like a high-stakes chess game where the board is the financial market and the pieces are your capital. You need strategy, foresight, and a deep understanding of risk and reward. So, let's demystify this complex yet fascinating financial instrument.

What Are Options?

An option is a contract that gives you the right—but not the obligation—to buy or sell an asset at a certain price before a specified expiration date. We've got two key players here: the "Call" and the "Put." A call option lets you buy an asset, and a put option lets you sell it. Seems simple, right? Hold on; the devil is in the details.

Calls: Your Ticket to the Upside

Let's say you're optimistic about Company X's stock, currently at $50. You buy a call option with a strike price of $55, expiring in a month. If the stock soars to $70, you can buy it at $55, thanks to your call option. You're in the money! But if the stock dips to $45 or stays below the strike price by the expiration date, your option becomes worthless. In the world of calls, timing and bullish sentiment are everything.

Puts: The Safety Net and More

Imagine you own shares of Company Y, which are currently worth $40 each. You're worried the price may drop, so you buy a put option with a $35 strike price. If the stock falls to $20, you can still sell it at $35. You've cushioned your fall. Puts are not just defensive; traders also use them to bet against stock performance. If you think Company Z's shares will plummet, you can buy a put and potentially make a profit from the stock's misfortune.

Premium: The Price of the Option

Nothing comes free in the financial markets, not even options. The price you pay for an option is called the premium. It's determined by various factors like the stock's volatility, time until expiration, and the difference between the stock and strike prices. And here's the catch: Even if the market doesn't move in your favor, the premium is non-refundable.

Time Decay: The Relentless Enemy

Options have expiration dates. As time ticks away, the option's value usually erodes, a phenomenon known as time decay. An option's time value is at its highest when purchased and usually diminishes as you near the expiration date. This is why long-term options are more expensive; they give you the luxury of time.

Leverage: The Double-Edged Sword

Options provide leverage, meaning you control a large amount of stock for a fraction of the cost. Leverage can magnify your profits, but remember, it amplifies your losses just as dramatically. You could lose your entire investment, the premium, if the market moves against you.

Risk Management: Protective Puts and Covered Calls

Options can also serve as an insurance policy for your portfolio. A protective put works as a hedge for your stock holdings, while a covered call can generate additional income. In a covered call, you sell a call option on stock you already own, pocketing the premium. However, you also risk having to sell the stock if it exceeds the strike price.

Taxes and Regulatory Nuances

Options have their own tax treatments and regulatory concerns. Short-term capital gains from options are generally taxed at a higher rate. It's crucial to understand these subtleties to avoid unpleasant surprises.

Ethical Dilemmas: The Short and Long of It

Shorting stocks using put options can be seen as profiting from a company's failure, which raises ethical questions. Additionally, excessive speculative options trading can contribute to market volatility. It's a grey area, and as an investor, you must tread carefully.

➔ The Grandmaster's Game

Option trading is a challenging, high-reward game of strategy, timing, and skill. While it offers a range of opportunities—from hedging risk to amplifying gains—the risks are just as varied. To become a grandmaster in this financial chess game, arm yourself with knowledge, planning, and an unyielding respect for the complexity of the market. It's your move.

4.3 Swaps: Interest Rate, Currency, and Commodity—The Art of Trading Risks

Swaps are financial instruments that often fly under the radar of mainstream investors, yet they represent one of the most ingenious ways to manage, trade, and capitalize on risk. Imagine a situation where you're good at managing variable interest rates, but terrible at handling fixed rates. There's someone else who faces the opposite challenge. What do you do? You swap. You trade your strengths and weaknesses to maximize efficiency. That's the core idea behind swaps.

The ABCs of Swaps

Let's start with the basics. A swap is a derivative contract between two parties to exchange financial obligations or cash flows. The most common types of swaps are interest rate, currency, and commodity swaps. Each has its own unique set of rules and purposes.

Interest Rate Swaps: Fixed for Variable, and Vice Versa

Imagine you're a company with a loan tied to a variable interest rate. You're having sleepless nights worrying about rate fluctuations. Across the street, another firm has a fixed-rate loan but wishes it could benefit from potentially falling rates. The solution? You swap your interest obligations. You agree to pay the fixed interest rate of the other company's loan, and they agree to cover your variable rate. Both of you hedge against the risks you're most concerned about. It's a win-win.

Currency Swaps: Navigating Forex Volatility

Picture this: a U.S. company wants to expand into Europe, while a European company aims to enter the U.S. market. Both are hesitant due to currency risks. They can enter into a currency swap, exchanging principal and interest payments in their respective currencies. This way, each company can manage revenue and expenses in a single currency, reducing foreign exchange risk.

Commodity Swaps: Locking in Prices

Commodity swaps are often the unsung heroes for industries dependent on raw materials like oil, gas, or metals. If an airline fears that jet fuel prices will skyrocket, it can enter into a swap with an oil producer. The airline agrees to pay a fixed rate for the fuel, while the producer commits to a variable rate tied to market prices. In essence, the airline hedges against rising prices, and the producer protects against falling ones.

The Pricing Mechanism: The Notional Amount

Swaps are generally structured around a 'notional amount,' which is the supposed amount upon which the cash flows are calculated. However, it's crucial to understand that this notional amount is never actually exchanged. It's a benchmark, a hypothetical figure used to compute the payments.

Counterparty Risk: The Elephant in the Room

Swaps can be fantastic tools for risk management, but they introduce a new hazard: counterparty risk. If the party you've swapped with defaults, you're left in the lurch. The collapse of Lehman Brothers in 2008 was a wake-up call for the dangers posed by counterparty risk in swap agreements.

Regulatory Oversight: From Wild West to Governed Territory

In the past, the swap market was like the Wild West—largely unregulated and opaque. Post-2008, entities like the Securities and Exchange Commission (SEC) and the Commodity Futures Trading Commission (CFTC) have stepped in to bring some order to this landscape.

Tax Implications: Yes, The Taxman Cares About Swaps

Swaps have their unique tax characteristics, with certain types of swaps being subject to the "60/40" rule in the U.S., where 60% of gains are taxed as long-term and 40% as short-term. Be sure you consult a tax advisor familiar with these nuances.

Ethical Considerations: Fair Game or Zero-Sum?

Swaps can sometimes be viewed as instruments that profit from another's loss, especially in speculative uses of interest rate or currency swaps. However, when used responsibly for hedging and risk management, they can be an integral part of a balanced financial ecosystem.

➔ Wrapping It Up: The Swiss Army Knife of Financial Instruments

Swaps are like the Swiss Army knife of the financial world. They have a tool for every need, be it managing interest rates, currencies, or commodities. However, with great power comes great responsibility. Swaps require a deep understanding of not just your own risk profile but also of market dynamics and the reliability of your counterparty. Done right, swaps are an art—the art of trading risks. So, are you ready to make a swap?

4.4 Exotic Derivatives: Asian Options, Barrier Options, etc.—The Enigmatic Instruments of Finance

When you hear the word 'exotic,' what comes to mind? Tropical beaches, rare animals, or perhaps luxurious cars? In the financial world, 'exotic' has a different connotation. It refers to complex, non-standard financial derivatives that go beyond your run-of-the-mill options and futures. While the term 'exotic' may imply something dangerous or risky, these derivatives are not necessarily riskier; they're just more intricate. So, let's pull back the curtain on some of these lesser-known instruments—Asian options, barrier options, and the like—to unravel their mystique.

Asian Options: Smooth Out the Kinks

Let's start with Asian options, which sound a lot more mysterious than they actually are. Unlike standard options that derive their value from the underlying asset's price at a specific point in time, Asian options use an average price over a period. Why? Smoothing. It's about tempering the highs and lows to reduce volatility. These are perfect for businesses that aren't concerned with immediate price but are more worried about the average cost over time. For instance, a company regularly importing raw materials might care more about the average monthly price rather than the daily fluctuations.

Barrier Options: The High-Stakes Gamble

Now, let's talk about barrier options. These are options that come to life or die based on the asset reaching a specific 'barrier' price. There are knock-in options, which activate only when the asset reaches a set price, and knock-out options, which deactivate if the asset hits a particular price. It's like playing a high-stakes video game, where you unlock levels or face game over based on your score. Barrier options are a great tool for hedging; for example, an investor can use a knock-out option to limit potential losses.

Lookback Options: Hindsight in a Contract

How many times have you wished for the benefit of hindsight in your investments? Lookback options almost make that wish come true. These options allow the holder to "look back" over time to determine the exercise price. In essence, you're allowed to capitalize on the most favorable price of the asset during a pre-determined period. Imagine buying a stock at its lowest point in the last three months; that's what a lookback option enables.

Rainbow Options: Multi-Asset, Multi-Potential

A rainbow option is a fascinating derivative linked to two or more underlying assets. Think of it as betting on a team rather than an individual player. They can be more affordable than buying multiple single-asset options and offer diversification, but they also come with the complexity of tracking multiple variables. These are commonly used in venture capital and infrastructure investments, where various factors can affect the outcome.

Digital Options: The Binary Bet

Digital options, often referred to as binary options, represent the most straightforward bet in the world of exotic derivatives. You predict whether an asset will be above or below a specific price at expiration. If you're right, you get a fixed payout; if you're wrong, you lose your investment. Simple as that.

Why Exotic Derivatives Exist: The Quest for Tailored Solutions

You might wonder, why do we even need these exotic derivatives? Can't we just stick to the basics? The answer lies in the inherent diversity of financial needs. Exotic derivatives offer customized solutions that more 'vanilla' financial instruments can't provide. These derivatives cater to specific risk profiles, market views, or operational needs, making them indispensable for informed financial engineering.

Risk and Reward

While exotic derivatives offer unique opportunities for risk management and profit, they are not without their perils. They often require a deep understanding of the underlying assets and market conditions, as well as the mathematical models used for pricing and risk assessment.

The Regulatory Labyrinth: Handle with Care

Due to their complexity, exotic derivatives are under stringent regulatory scrutiny. Misuse or misunderstanding can have severe consequences, both financial and legal. Always make sure you're complying with the regulations relevant to your jurisdiction before diving into these complex waters.

➔ **The Spice of Financial Life**

In a nutshell, exotic derivatives are the spices in the financial stew. They add flavor and complexity, catering to specialized tastes and needs. But like any potent spice, they must be used judiciously. Mastering exotic derivatives requires both knowledge and caution. If you're willing to put in the effort to understand their complexities, they can be an incredibly powerful addition to your financial toolkit.

5. MONEY MARKETS

5.1 Treasury Bills: The Cornerstone of Low-Risk Investment

If you're looking for the ultimate low-risk investment, look no further than Treasury Bills, often abbreviated as T-Bills. These unassuming pieces of paper—or more commonly, electronic entries—are like the bedrock upon which the financial world rests. When everything else in the economy seems shaky, T-Bills are the closest thing to a sure bet. Why? Because they are backed by the full faith and credit of the United States government.

The Basics: What Exactly Are Treasury Bills?

Treasury Bills are short-term debt instruments issued by the U.S. Department of the Treasury. They come with maturities that range from a few days to 52 weeks. Unlike bonds, they don't pay interest in the traditional sense. Instead, you buy them at a discount to their face value. For instance, you might buy a $1,000 T-Bill for $980. When it matures, you get back the full $1,000. That $20 difference is essentially your interest, and that's how you make money.

The Auction House: How T-Bills Are Sold

T-Bills are sold in regular auctions, and there are two types: competitive and non-competitive. In a competitive auction, you specify the yield (interest rate) you're willing to accept, and you may not receive any T-Bills if your bid is too low. In a non-competitive auction, you agree to accept whatever yield is determined, ensuring that you get the T-Bill. This flexibility allows investors from all walks of life to participate, from the individual looking to park some emergency funds to the massive institutional investors.

Risk-Free Rate: The Benchmark for All Other Investments
The interest rate on a Treasury Bill is often referred to as the "risk-free rate," and it serves as a benchmark for all other interest rates in the economy. When you hear financial pundits talking about rates going up or down, they're often tacitly referring to the movement of the T-Bill rate. Why? Because if the government—the most secure borrower—has to pay more or less to borrow money, you can bet everyone else will too.

Liquidity Galore: Turn Them Into Cash—Fast!
One of the key advantages of T-Bills is their liquidity. Because they're so secure and so widely traded, you can easily sell them on the secondary market before they mature. This makes T-Bills an excellent option for anyone who might need quick access to their cash.

Yield Curve Insights: What T-Bills Tell Us
Pay attention to the Treasury yield curve, which plots the yields of T-Bills of different maturities. A "normal" upward-sloping curve means the economy is doing well. But if the curve "inverts," with shorter-term yields higher than longer-term ones, watch out; it's often a harbinger of economic downturns.

Inflation Woes: The Achilles' Heel
Now, they're not entirely without risk. The yield generally tracks along with inflation, but if inflation spikes suddenly, your real return could be negative. However, for the most part, they're as secure as you can get in the often unpredictable world of investments.

Tax Benefits: Some Silver Linings

Here's another nugget: while the interest you earn is subject to federal income tax, it's exempt from state and local taxes. That's a feature not commonly found in other investments and can make T-Bills slightly more attractive in high-tax states.

The Global Perspective: A Universal Safe Haven

It's not just Americans who flock to T-Bills; they are globally considered a safe haven asset. In times of international crisis, global investors often buy up U.S. T-Bills, considering them safer than their own country's debt or other investment options.

➔ The Trusty Financial Cushion

So we can say that Treasury Bills are your financial security blanket. They offer unmatched safety, reasonable returns, and incredible liquidity. They're the intro class in the school of investments, yet they're also a staple in the portfolios of the most sophisticated investors. Whether you're looking to safeguard your money, park funds for a short term, or even engage in more complex trading strategies like arbitrage, T-Bills are a cornerstone asset that can meet multiple needs. Investing in them is almost like putting your money in a fortress that guards against the volatility of the financial markets. So, if you're looking to take a step into the world of investing without taking on too much risk, T-Bills should be your starting point.

5.2 Repos and Reverse Repos: The Financial Plumbing You Never Knew You Needed

If you thought Treasury Bills were the bread and butter of the financial markets, brace yourself for Repos and Reverse Repos— the unsung heroes that keep the financial markets lubricated and running smoothly. Trust me, these aren't just Wall Street jargon; they're foundational pieces in the architecture of modern finance. And they happen every single day, right under your nose.

What Are Repos and Reverse Repos Anyway?
Let's start with the basics. "Repo" is short for repurchase agreement. In a Repo, one party sells an asset (usually a Treasury security) to another party with an agreement to repurchase it later, typically overnight, at a slightly higher price. The difference in price represents the interest. Now, flip the perspective, and you get a Reverse Repo. The buyer in a Repo becomes the seller in a Reverse Repo, agreeing to sell the asset back later. It's the same transaction, just viewed from the other side.

The Overnight Market: Financial Whac-A-Mole
Picture this: Banks have cash reserves that fluctuate daily due to customer transactions. Some end up with excess reserves, while others face a shortfall. Rather than letting these funds sit idle or experience a deficit, banks lend to each other overnight through Repos and Reverse Repos. This helps to iron out short-term imbalances, making the whole system more efficient. Essentially, it's financial Whac-A-Mole, ensuring that no bank is left with too much or too little.

Central Bank's Toolbox: Steering the Ship

If you think this is just a playground for banks, think again. Central banks like the Federal Reserve use Repos and Reverse Repos to steer short-term interest rates, affecting the cost of borrowing throughout the economy. When the Fed wants to inject money into the system, it buys assets in Repo transactions. When it wants to pull money out, it sells assets in Reverse Repo transactions. It's like the steering wheel of the economy, making tiny adjustments to keep us on course.

Risk: The Shadow on the Wall

Now, let's talk about the elephant in the room: risk. Compared to other financial instruments, Repos are relatively low-risk. The short duration—often just overnight—reduces the chance of something going catastrophically wrong. Plus, the assets involved are usually low-risk securities like Treasuries. However, there's still counterparty risk. If one party fails to fulfill their end of the bargain, it can trigger a chain reaction in the financial system. It's a shadow on the wall that's worth watching but rarely manifests into something more sinister.

Benefits for Individual Investors: Not Just a Big Boys' Game

Repos aren't exclusive to financial giants. Money market funds, for example, often engage in Reverse Repos to park their cash safely and earn a little interest. Some brokerages even allow individual investors to lend out securities in a similar manner, though this is less common. The point is, Repos indirectly affect you whether you're aware of it or not.

Impact on Liquidity: The Unsung Hero

Above all, Repos and Reverse Repos are about liquidity—keeping cash and assets flowing smoothly through the system. Imagine a city's water supply; you don't notice it until something goes wrong. The same applies here. When Repos function as they should, they're almost invisible, yet they're essential for a stable, functioning financial market.

Regulatory Measures: The Watchful Eye

Given their critical role, Repos are subject to oversight. Regulators aim to make the Repo market more transparent and resilient, particularly in the wake of financial crises where the Repo market has shown its vulnerabilities. This keeps the financial plumbing robust and minimizes systemic risks.

➔ A Balancing Act: Keeping the Scales Even

Repos and Reverse Repos are the balancing act that keeps financial markets stable. They help banks, serve as a tool for central banks, and even offer options for individual investors. These transactions might seem insignificant due to their short-term nature, but their cumulative impact is colossal. The next time you hear about interest rates or wonder how banks manage their daily reserves, remember the quiet yet essential role of Repos and Reverse Repos. Because without them, the whole financial system would be a lot shakier than it is today.

5.3 Money Market Funds: The Swiss Army Knife of Finance

Let's talk about Money Market Funds, the financial world's version of a Swiss Army knife: versatile, reliable, and often underestimated. Whether you're an individual looking to park some cash or a corporation needing short-term liquidity, these funds offer something for everyone. You'll find them nestled within the broader landscape of money markets, but make no mistake—they're not your garden-variety investment tool.

The Basics: More Than a Savings Account

First, let's dispel some myths. Despite the name, Money Market Funds are not the same as money market accounts you might have at your local bank. They are investment funds that buy highly liquid, short-term instruments like Treasury bills and commercial paper. They aim to maintain a constant net asset value (NAV), typically at $1 per share, making them seemingly as safe as a bank account. But remember, they are not FDIC-insured, even if they feel like a glorified savings account.

The Real MVP: Liquidity

Why are these funds so crucial? One word: liquidity. In a world where businesses and individuals alike need quick access to cash without a fuss, Money Market Funds are the go-to option. They offer the trifecta: safety, liquidity, and a smidgen of interest—far more than your standard checking account but less than long-term investments.

Corporations and Money Market Funds: A Love Story

Here's a revelation: Many corporations hoard cash in Money Market Funds. Why? Imagine you're a company that just sold a mountain of goods and suddenly have a pile of cash. You need somewhere to put it—somewhere safe and accessible. Enter Money Market Funds. They're the corporate equivalent of stuffing money under the mattress, but with interest.

Retail Investors, You're Not Left Out

But let's not forget individual investors. If you've got some cash and don't know where to invest it temporarily, Money Market Funds are your friend. They're a great holding area, especially if you're between investments or saving for a short-term goal.

The Safety Quotient: Not Zero Risk, But Close

Here's where people often get tripped up. Money Market Funds feel safe—and they largely are—but they're not entirely risk-free. They invest in high-quality, short-term debt, but there's always the slim possibility of something going awry. The financial crisis of 2008 proved that when the Reserve Primary Fund "broke the buck," meaning its NAV dropped below $1. Panic ensued, and reforms were made to improve the resiliency of these funds. The risk is minimal but not nonexistent.

Navigating the Types: Prime, Government, and Municipal

Think all Money Market Funds are the same? Think again. There are different flavors—Prime Funds, which invest in commercial paper and are typically for institutional investors; Government Funds, which invest mostly in U.S. Treasuries and are the epitome of safety; and Municipal Funds, which offer tax benefits but come with slightly higher risk.

Yield and Expense Ratios: The Devil is in the Details

Before you dive in, pay attention to the yield and the expense ratio. Yield is the interest you'll earn, often quoted as a seven-day annualized yield. The expense ratio is what you pay the fund manager. A high expense ratio can eat into your earnings, turning a seemingly attractive yield into a mediocre one.

Regulatory Watchdogs: The Gatekeepers

Don't worry; regulators keep a close eye on these funds. Post-2008 reforms require funds to maintain liquidity buffers and disclose more information. The aim is to prevent runs and keep the market stable.

➔ The Utility Player in Your Portfolio

Money Market Funds are the utility players in your financial portfolio. They may not hit home runs in terms of returns, but they're reliable, flexible, and can fill multiple roles. So, the next time you're contemplating where to park some cash, whether for corporate or personal needs, don't overlook the Swiss Army knife of finance that is the Money Market Fund. After all, it's the unsung hero that adds a layer of safety, liquidity, and efficiency to your financial endeavors.

6. RISK MANAGEMENT

6.1 Hedging Strategies: Your Financial Safety Net

Life is fraught with uncertainty, and so are financial markets. You've built a portfolio, made investments, and now, like a parent watching their child ride a bike for the first time, you're anxious. Will your investments take a hit? Will the market conditions turn unfavorable? This is where hedging strategies come in, acting as your financial safety net, ready to catch you if you fall.

Why Hedge? Because No One Can Predict the Future

Hedging isn't about making money; it's about protecting what you already have. Imagine you've built a castle out of your investments. Hedging is the moat around it. No one knows what storms the future holds, but if one comes, wouldn't you rather have some protection in place?

The Basics: What's a Hedge?

In the simplest terms, a hedge is an investment that's intended to offset potential losses from another investment. If you own shares of Company A, and you're worried those shares might lose value, you can 'hedge' by investing in a financial instrument that will gain value if Company A's stock declines.

Types of Hedging Strategies: The Tools at Your Disposal

There are myriad ways to hedge, and the method you choose will depend on what exactly you're trying to protect. Here are some of the most common types:

Future Contracts: Lock in the Price Now

Futures contracts allow you to lock in the price of an asset you'll buy or sell in the future. Use this if you're a business worried about fluctuating commodity prices.

Options: The Right, Not Obligation, to Buy or Sell

Options give you the right to buy or sell an asset at a certain price before a certain date. It's like paying a premium for car insurance, but for your investments.

Short Selling: Profit from the Downfall

In a short sale, you borrow shares to sell them, hoping to buy them back at a lower price later. Use this if you believe a particular asset will decline in value.

Diversification: Don't Put All Your Eggs in One Basket

Yes, diversification is a form of hedging. By spreading your investments across various assets or sectors, you mitigate the risk associated with any single investment tanking.

Hedging Costs Money: Accept the Trade-Off

Hedging isn't free. Whether it's the premium for an options contract or the interest on borrowed shares for a short sale, you'll pay something. And when your hedge works, it often means that your original investment didn't. It's the financial equivalent of buying an umbrella because you think it's going to rain; if you end up needing it, it means you're caught in the rain.

Hedging Isn't Just for Wall Street

While it's a popular tool for big financial institutions, even individual investors can benefit from hedging. Thanks to various financial instruments and options available in the market today, it's never been easier for retail investors to protect their portfolios.

The Risks: Hedging Isn't Foolproof

It's vital to remember that hedging is not a guarantee against loss. Ineffective hedging strategies can lead to losses, sometimes exacerbating the very risks they were designed to mitigate. Always do your homework before you hedge. Understand the costs, the potential outcomes, and make sure the hedge is appropriate for the risk you're trying to offset.

➔ The Moral of the Story: Be Prepared

If there's one takeaway from this, it's that you should always be prepared. Hedging is about managing risk, not avoiding it. It allows you to make more precise decisions about what risks you should take, which is what investing is all about. So, go on, build your castle of investments, but don't forget to dig that moat. With the right hedging strategies, you can safeguard your financial future and sleep a little easier at night, knowing you've done your best to protect your wealth.

6.2 Risk Assessment and Ratings: The Yardstick of Financial Security

Let's not beat around the bush: you're diving into the world of financial instruments because you aim to grow your wealth. But how do you know if you're jumping into a pool or off a cliff? That's where risk assessment and ratings step in, serving as your financial GPS, guiding you on the path of least resistance—or at least, lesser risk.

What's Risk, Anyway?

First things first, risk isn't necessarily bad; it's the potential for loss. Without risk, there's no reward. But blindly diving into risk is as wise as walking into a maze blindfolded. You need a yardstick to measure this elusive concept, and that's where risk assessment and ratings come in.

Risk Assessment: Your Financial Health Check-up

Think of risk assessment as a full-body scan for your investment. It gauges various factors like market conditions, issuer credibility, economic indicators, and so forth. Imagine you're about to invest in a company's stock. The risk assessment will scan everything from the company's financials to the industry's future prospects.

How It's Done

Various methodologies exist for risk assessment, but they usually break down into two categories: quantitative and qualitative. Quantitative analysis is all about numbers—profit margins, debt levels, and market share. Qualitative analysis focuses on less tangible factors like brand reputation or regulatory environment. Effective risk assessment combines both.

Ratings: The Grades of the Financial World

Once an assessment is complete, you often get a risk rating. These ratings are shorthand indicators of an investment's risk level, courtesy of rating agencies like Moody's, Standard & Poor's, and Fitch.

Investment-Grade vs. Junk

Here's where it gets juicy. Ratings classify investments as either "investment-grade" or "junk." Investment-grade assets are the teacher's pets of the financial world—low risk but often with lower yields. Junk assets are the rebels—higher risk but potentially higher rewards.

Why You Should Care

You're not gambling; you're investing. Knowing the risk level helps you allocate your resources wisely. Imagine a balanced diet; you wouldn't eat just candy or just salads. A well-balanced portfolio mixes various risk levels to achieve a blend of safety and potential for high returns.

Individual vs. Institutional Investors

Now, if you think risk assessment and ratings are only for the big players or institutional investors, think again. With the democratization of finance, even retail investors have access to sophisticated risk assessment tools. Websites and apps offer user-friendly interfaces to analyze and interpret these complex assessments, making it easier for you to make informed decisions.

Caveats: Ratings Aren't Gospel

It's essential to note that ratings aren't infallible. Agencies have been wrong before, and a high rating today doesn't guarantee it'll remain high tomorrow. Always conduct your own due diligence.

The Future: AI and Risk Assessment

A word on what's coming: Artificial Intelligence is making inroads into risk assessment, offering real-time analysis that accounts for a myriad of variables. This isn't some sci-fi movie plot; it's a rapidly evolving reality that will revolutionize how we assess investment risk.

➔ Knowledge Is Power

Ignorance isn't bliss when your hard-earned money is on the line. Risk assessment and ratings aren't crystal balls, but they're the next best thing. They provide a quantifiable, understandable measure of what you're getting into, helping you invest wisely rather than gamble blindly. So the next time you're about to leap into a new investment opportunity, pause. Take a moment to understand the risk, consult the ratings, and weigh your options. Your future self, enjoying the fruits of well-calculated risks, will thank you.

7. VALUATION

7.1 Discounted Cash Flows (DCF): The Crystal Ball of Finance

If you're genuinely serious about making sound investment decisions, there's one tool you absolutely can't ignore—Discounted Cash Flows, or DCF. Think of it as your financial crystal ball, the closest you'll get to seeing the future value of an investment. And before you start yawning about complicated financial jargon, hear me out: understanding DCF could mean the difference between buying a treasure chest or a ticking time bomb.

What Is DCF?

At its core, DCF tells you what money you can expect to make from an investment is worth in today's terms. Why? Because a dollar today is worth more than a dollar tomorrow, thanks to inflation, risks, and opportunity costs. You could invest that dollar elsewhere and potentially make more money. The DCF method uses this principle to bring future cash flows back to their present value, providing a single figure that summarizes the "worthiness" of an investment.

How to Perform a DCF Analysis

Now, the mechanics. You'll be dealing with two main components: future cash flows and the discount rate. Future cash flows are what you expect to earn from the investment, while the discount rate is essentially the rate of return you'd require to make the investment worth it.

Future Cash Flows

This part requires a crystal ball—or a close substitute: thorough research. You'll need to forecast how much cash the investment will generate. For a business, look at things like earnings projections, revenue growth, and other financial statements.

Discount Rate

This is where you define your expectations. The discount rate reflects the time value of money and the risk of the investment. A higher discount rate means you expect more from the investment, making it harder for the asset to have a high present value. You'll often hear terms like 'Weighted Average Cost of Capital (WACC)' in this context. Don't let that spook you—it's just a more nuanced way to set the discount rate.

The Math: Don't Panic

The formula might look intimidating, but it's not as bad as it seems. You take each future cash flow and discount it back to its present value using the formula:

$$DCF = \frac{CF1}{(1+r)^\wedge 1} + \frac{CF2}{(1+r)^\wedge 2} + \frac{CFn}{(1+r)^\wedge n}$$

Where *CF* is the cash flow and *r* is the discount rate.

Why DCF is the Gold Standard

DCF is widely used for a reason. It considers both the risk and time value of money, providing a comprehensive picture of an investment's value. This is invaluable in multiple sectors, from equities and real estate to corporate budgeting.

The Pitfalls: Garbage In, Garbage Out

Look, no tool is perfect. DCF relies heavily on the quality of your inputs. Bad assumptions about future cash flows or discount rates can lead to misleading results. The future is uncertain, and no one can predict it with 100% accuracy. But what DCF does is force you to make your assumptions explicit. It makes you think critically about why you expect certain outcomes, which is already half the battle in making a good investment.

Real-world Applications

The power of DCF isn't limited to Wall Street wizards or finance gurus. Anyone considering buying a property, starting a business, or even valuing a potential job offer can use DCF to evaluate the true value of the opportunity in front of them.

DCF in the Age of Uncertainty

Yes, we're in turbulent times—political upheavals, economic swings, and even global pandemics. All these affect future cash flows and discount rates. But rather than making DCF irrelevant, this uncertainty makes it even more crucial. By forcing you to consider various scenarios and how they would affect your investment, DCF equips you to be a more resilient and adaptable investor.

➔ **The Bottom Line: Your Financial Crystal Ball**

DCF is your key to unlocking the mysteries of an investment's true worth. It's not just a formula; it's a mindset that pushes you to understand the nitty-gritty of your investment, the risks involved, and what you stand to gain. When applied diligently and thoughtfully, DCF can be the guardian angel that steers you away from bad investments and towards opportunities that are genuinely worth your time and money.

7.2 Relative Valuation Methods: The Unsung Heroes of Financial Decision-Making

You've already read about Discounted Cash Flows (DCF), the finance world's darling. Now, it's time for the unsung heroes: Relative Valuation Methods. These are your go-to techniques when you don't have a crystal ball to forecast cash flows, or when you simply don't have the time for complex calculations. They're fast, they're intuitive, and they can still get you some incredibly accurate results.

What Is Relative Valuation?

In the simplest terms, relative valuation involves comparing the value of one asset to similar assets in the market. If you were buying a house, you'd naturally compare its price to similar houses in the neighborhood, right? Well, relative valuation methods do precisely that, but for financial assets like stocks, bonds, or entire businesses.

Why Does It Matter?

Don't underestimate the power of relative valuation. In many real-world scenarios—especially in fast-moving markets—DCF is cumbersome. You often don't have the luxury of time to sit down and calculate the net present value of every future cash flow. That's where relative valuation shines. It provides a quick and dirty way to gauge an asset's value, making it incredibly useful for investors, traders, and analysts.

The Tools: Multiples and Ratios

The workhorses of relative valuation are the multiples and ratios you've probably heard about—Price-to-Earnings (P/E), Price-to-Book (P/B), Enterprise Value-to-EBITDA, and so on. Each of these metrics provides a unique lens through which to evaluate an asset.

Price-to-Earnings (P/E)
This is the golden boy of stock valuation. A low P/E ratio could indicate that the stock is undervalued, while a high P/E might suggest overvaluation. The key is to compare it with P/E ratios of companies in the same sector.

Price-to-Book (P/B)
Here's another heavyweight. If you're dealing with asset-heavy companies like banks or real estate firms, P/B can be more reliable than P/E. A P/B ratio under 1 might indicate that the stock is undervalued relative to its assets, but as always, comparisons are key.

Enterprise Value-to-EBITDA
This is the go-to multiple when you're evaluating entire companies, especially during mergers or acquisitions. It takes into account both the equity and debt, providing a fuller picture of a company's value.

The Methodology: Comparable Companies Analysis (CCA)

The concept is dead simple: find similar companies, look at their multiples, and apply them to the company you're interested in. This is often done through a Comparable Companies Analysis (CCA). You'll hear this term tossed around a lot in investment banking and equity research. It's straightforward but highly effective.

The Caveats: No Free Lunch

As with anything in finance, relative valuation methods are not without their pitfalls. For starters, finding truly comparable companies can be a Herculean task. Markets are dynamic, and companies evolve. And let's not forget about differences in growth rates, risk profiles, and competitive advantages, which can all skew your multiples.

The Hybrid Approach: Best of Both Worlds

Let's be clear: you shouldn't use relative valuation in isolation. The smart move is to use it in conjunction with other methods like DCF. This hybrid approach can give you a fuller, more nuanced understanding of an asset's value. It's like getting a second opinion on a critical medical diagnosis—you'll feel more confident about your decisions.

➔ Don't Ignore Relative Valuation

So here's the deal. Relative valuation methods may not have the glamour and complexity of DCF, but they're indispensable tools in your financial toolkit. They offer quick insights, they're easy to use, and they provide a different perspective on value that can save you from making costly mistakes. Like the dependable sidekick in a buddy movie, they may not grab the headlines, but they sure do make the hero look good. And in the world of finance, who doesn't want to look good?

7.3 Option Pricing Models: The Rosetta Stones of Derivative Markets

No, they're not some mystical formulas cooked up in a finance lab, although they might as well be. These are the Rosetta Stones of the derivative markets, decoding the perplexing world of options into numbers you can actually understand and, more importantly, use.

The Basics: What Are Options?

Let's set the stage by quickly revisiting what options are. An option is essentially a contract that gives you the right—but not the obligation—to buy or sell an asset at a certain price within a specified period. Easy enough? Good. Now let's talk about how to price these things.

The Powerhouses: Black-Scholes and Binomial Models

The Black-Scholes and Binomial models are the two grandmasters of option pricing. If you've even taken a cursory look at finance, you've likely stumbled upon the Black-Scholes formula. Developed by three economists—Fisher Black, Myron Scholes, and Robert Merton—this mathematical marvel won Scholes and Merton a Nobel Prize. The Binomial model, while not as sexy, is an incredibly effective tool that uses a more simplified, step-by-step approach to option pricing.

Black-Scholes Model

This model crams a bunch of factors into a single formula: stock price, strike price, time until expiration, risk-free rate, and volatility. Plug them in, do some calculus, and voila—you have your option price. It's particularly useful for European options, which can only be exercised at expiration.

Binomial Model

The Binomial model, on the other hand, uses a tree-like structure to show all possible paths an option's price could take. It's more versatile than Black-Scholes and is excellent for American options, which can be exercised at any time before expiration. The more steps in your binomial tree, the more accurate your pricing will be.

Why You Should Care: Real-world Applications

Ever wonder how hedge funds and trading firms make (or lose) millions on options? Well, it all starts with accurate pricing. If you know what an option is truly worth, you can make informed decisions about buying, selling, or holding. Option pricing models provide that critical insight. These models are your roadmap in the complex, often convoluted world of derivative markets.

The Caveats: Model Limitations

Okay, real talk. As awesome as these models are, they're not infallible. The Black-Scholes model assumes constant volatility and interest rates, which we all know is about as likely as a snowstorm in the Sahara. The Binomial model, while more flexible, becomes computationally intense with more steps. Plus, both models can be sensitive to input changes, which means a small error can lead to big mispricings.

A New Age: Modern Extensions

Financial engineers (yes, that's a real job) are continually fine-tuning these models to adapt to today's fast-paced, algorithm-driven markets. Stochastic volatility models, like the Heston model, and jump diffusion models aim to fix some of the gaps left by Black-Scholes and Binomial. These are the next frontier in option pricing, helping investors navigate increasingly complex financial landscapes.

➔ Your Financial Toolbox Needs These Models

So why does any of this matter to you? Because understanding option pricing models is like learning the rules of chess. You can't play the game effectively if you don't know how the pieces move. Whether you're an individual investor, a finance student, or a Wall Street veteran, these models offer valuable, actionable insights. They help you assess risk, devise strategies, and ultimately, make more informed financial decisions. So... don't underestimate the power of option pricing models. They might look intimidating with their Greek letters and intricate formulas, but once you crack the code, you've got a potent weapon in your financial arsenal. They're the keys to deciphering market behaviors, opening up a world of trading and investment opportunities that you'd be foolish to ignore.

8. REGULATION AND COMPLIANCE

8.1 Securities and Exchange Commission (SEC): The Financial World's Watchdog

If you're dabbling in the world of financial instruments, you'd better get acquainted with the Securities and Exchange Commission (SEC). Why? Because like it or not, this is the agency that holds the strings, the referee that calls the fouls, and the watchdog that's making sure nobody's playing dirty in the U.S. financial markets.

The What and the Why: Understanding the SEC's Role

Founded in 1934 as part of the New Deal to restore trust in the market after the Great Depression, the SEC's mission is to protect investors, maintain fair, orderly, and efficient markets, and facilitate capital formation. In short, they're here to make sure that when you buy a stock or bond, you're not buying into a sham.

The Bread and Butter: Regulations

The SEC loves its regulations, and there are tons of them. We're talking about laws like the Securities Act of 1933, the Securities Exchange Act of 1934, and let's not forget the Investment Advisers Act of 1940. These acts form the foundation of U.S. securities law. They dictate what companies must disclose, who can trade, and what constitutes fraudulent activity.

Registration and Disclosure

One of the SEC's main jobs is to ensure companies disclose the right information when they go public or issue new securities. The agency scrutinizes the registration statements and financial reports that companies are obliged to provide. Why? So you, the investor, have the facts to make informed decisions.

Market Oversight

The SEC also oversees broker-dealers, investment advisors, mutual funds, and even some elements of the blockchain and cryptocurrency world. It works in tandem with other organizations like the Financial Industry Regulatory Authority (FINRA) to oversee the entire trading landscape. So, think of the SEC as the captain of a complex, ever-changing team of financial regulators.

The Enforcer: Cracking Down on Malpractice

If you're thinking of insider trading or cooking the books, think again. The SEC has a track record of imposing severe penalties on companies and individuals who cross the line. Remember the Enron scandal? Or how about Bernie Madoff? The SEC was the entity responsible for bringing these cases to light and taking action, albeit with some criticisms about its effectiveness and timing.

The Watchful Eye: How It Affects You

As an investor, trader, or even just a casual market observer, the SEC affects your life more than you may realize. Its rules influence what kind of information companies have to reveal, affecting your ability to make informed investment decisions. If you're an entrepreneur looking to go public, the SEC's regulations will be your new bible. Essentially, the SEC aims to level the playing field, so the markets are less of a rigged game and more of a fair competition.

The Dark Side: Criticisms and Limitations

Let's be honest. The SEC isn't perfect. It's been criticized for being both overzealous and toothless at different times. Some argue it stifles innovation with excessive regulation, while others say it fails to catch fraudsters quickly enough. Yet, despite its imperfections, the SEC remains the most powerful financial regulatory agency in the U.S. and a model for many countries around the world.

➔ It's Your Financial Lifeguard

The SEC may have its flaws, but let's not forget its essential role in maintaining market integrity. Whether you're buying stocks, bonds, or dabbling in derivatives, the SEC is the lifeguard at the beach of financial markets. And while it may not catch every rogue wave or undercurrent, it's a crucial force aiming to keep you from drowning in scams, bad deals, and poor financial decisions. So... if you're navigating the turbulent waters of financial instruments, it pays—quite literally—to know how the SEC operates, what it monitors, and why it matters to you. Understanding the SEC's role in the financial ecosystem is not just optional; it's mandatory for anyone serious about investing or participating in capital markets. So, consider this a fundamental chapter in your financial education. After all, in the high-stakes world of finance, it's always better to be safe, informed, and, above all, SEC-compliant.

8.2 Financial Industry Regulatory Authority (FINRA): The Unsung Hero of Market Integrity

When we talk about financial market regulation, most people immediately think of the Securities and Exchange Commission (SEC). But let's pull back the curtain on another key player you absolutely need to know: the Financial Industry Regulatory Authority, or FINRA. While the SEC often steals the limelight, FINRA plays an equally critical role, although it operates in the shadows to keep your investments safe and markets honest.

Who is FINRA?

FINRA is a non-governmental organization that regulates member brokerage firms and exchange markets. Founded in 2007 from the consolidation of the National Association of Securities Dealers (NASD) and the regulation and enforcement arms of the New York Stock Exchange, FINRA operates under the supervision of the SEC. It's tasked with one overriding goal: to safeguard the integrity of the markets and protect investors like you and me.

What FINRA Does: Compliance and Licensing

One of FINRA's main jobs is ensuring compliance. They write and enforce rules governing the ethical activities of all registered broker-dealer firms in the United States. If you're a broker or planning to become one, you'll have to pass FINRA-administered exams to become licensed. And it's not a one-time affair; FINRA monitors its members continually, ensuring that they adhere to federal securities laws and FINRA's own regulations.

Market Surveillance: The Eye in the Sky

FINRA keeps a watchful eye on the market. Using sophisticated technology, they track irregularities and potential fraud schemes in real-time. If a particular stock exhibits strange trading patterns or volumes, FINRA is the one to flag it and investigate. This level of scrutiny helps maintain an even playing field for all market participants.

Disciplinary Actions: The Iron Fist in the Velvet Glove

When FINRA finds violations, they don't mess around. The authority has the power to levy fines, suspend brokers, and even bar firms and individuals from the industry. You might not hear about these actions as much as you do about the SEC's high-profile cases, but rest assured, FINRA's disciplinary measures are a cornerstone in upholding market integrity.

Public Resources: Empowering the Investor

But FINRA isn't just about rules and enforcement. They also provide invaluable resources to educate the public. Through databases like BrokerCheck, you can investigate the background of brokers and investment advisors before entrusting them with your hard-earned money. Tools like these make FINRA not just a regulator but also an advocate for investors.

Why FINRA Matters to You

Whether you're an active trader or a long-term investor, FINRA's work affects you. It's their relentless scrutiny that adds a layer of safety, making sure that the brokers you deal with are qualified and ethical. The rules and guidelines they set dictate the level of service and fairness you can expect in your financial dealings.

The Critical Partnership: FINRA and SEC

Many often confuse the roles of FINRA and the SEC, thinking they might be competitors or substitutes for each other. They're not. They work in tandem. While the SEC has a broad mandate that includes various aspects of the financial industry, FINRA specializes in overseeing brokerage firms and their registered representatives. This relationship allows for a comprehensive and nuanced approach to market regulation.

The Verdict: Your Silent Guardian

While FINRA might not make headlines as often as the SEC, its work is integral to the functioning of transparent, fair financial markets in the United States. Knowing that a specialized entity is keeping tabs on brokerage activities should give you an extra layer of confidence when participating in the market.

So, if you're serious about investing or making a career in finance, understanding FINRA is non-negotiable. This regulatory body shapes the landscape of modern finance, ensuring it remains a realm of opportunity rather than a den of inequity.

➔ To sum it up, FINRA might be the unsung hero of financial regulation, but its impact is nothing short of monumental. Whether you're an investor, a broker, or someone considering a dive into the financial markets, FINRA is a name you should know and respect. Because in the complex, sometimes murky waters of finance, it's often the quiet regulators like FINRA who make the most noise when it comes to keeping things on the up and up.

8.3 International Regulatory Bodies: The Global Watchdogs You've Never Heard Of

In a world where finance knows no borders, focusing solely on domestic regulators like the SEC and FINRA is akin to playing checkers while everyone else is playing 3D chess. We can't talk about financial regulation without delving into the international arena. If the U.S. agencies are the local sheriffs, then meet the global police force: the international regulatory bodies that govern financial markets.

Meet the Squad: The Big Names in International Regulation

First off, let's introduce the all-stars. Ever heard of the International Monetary Fund (IMF)? How about the World Bank? These are the titans that often make headlines, but there's also a set of lesser-known, specialized agencies like the Basel Committee on Banking Supervision (BCBS), the Financial Stability Board (FSB), and the International Organization of Securities Commissions (IOSCO). These organizations aim to bring order and standardization to the global financial circus.

What's the Big Deal with Basel?

Let's zero in on the Basel Committee. Originating in the quaint Swiss city of Basel, this committee is anything but provincial. It sets the international standards for banking regulation, including the critical Basel Accords that dictate how much capital banks must hold. Why should you care? Because the Basel rules are often the backbone of your local banking regulations. If Basel sneezes, the global financial system could catch a cold.

FSB: The Think Tank with Teeth

Next up, the Financial Stability Board. This international body monitors and makes recommendations to ensure global financial stability. But don't be fooled by the term "recommendations." When the FSB speaks, policymakers listen. The FSB played a key role in post-2008 reforms, including rules on shadow banking and over-the-counter derivatives. In simple terms, the FSB makes sure that the financial crisis movie doesn't get a sequel.

IOSCO: The Protector of Your Portfolio

Now let's talk about IOSCO, a key player in the regulation of securities markets. While individual countries have their own securities regulators, like the SEC in the U.S., IOSCO aims to harmonize these regulations. It's like the United Nations of securities markets. From protecting investors to ensuring markets are fair, efficient, and transparent, IOSCO lays down the international law.

Beyond the Alphabet Soup: The Real Impact

Still wondering why these agencies matter to you? Consider this: in today's interconnected financial landscape, a ripple in one part of the world can become a tsunami elsewhere. Remember the 2008 financial crisis? It didn't just stay in Wall Street; it spread like wildfire globally. That's why these international bodies are crucial. They're the firefighters, and they're trying to make sure the whole forest doesn't go up in flames.

Not All Roses: The Challenges

That said, it's not smooth sailing for these international regulators. Sovereignty is a thorny issue. Countries often guard their financial markets like family jewels and are skeptical about ceding control to international bodies. Implementing and enforcing international rules is a Herculean task that requires consensus, something not easily achieved in the global arena.

Global Player or Local Fan? You Can't Afford to Ignore

Whether you're a globetrotting investor or someone who prefers to keep their money closer to home, understanding the role of international regulatory bodies is non-negotiable. Even if you invest solely in domestic markets, the regulations set by these international bodies trickle down to your local regulators and, ultimately, affect your portfolio's safety and performance.

➔ **Know Your Global Watchdogs**

So, it's high time you got acquainted with these faceless entities shaping the landscape of international finance. Their impact is often invisible but unmistakably massive. They set the rules of the game, ensure fair play, and strive for a stable and transparent global financial system. In a world where financial news crosses oceans in milliseconds, these international regulatory bodies are not just optional background knowledge; they are essential players that you must understand to truly grasp the global financial system. Ignore them at your peril, for in the vast, intricate world of global finance, these regulators are the linchpins that hold it all together.

9. MARKET ANALYSIS

9.1 Technical Analysis: The Unseen Patterns That Drive the Market

If you've ever heard someone say, "The trend is your friend," then you've already touched the tip of the iceberg that is technical analysis. But here's the big reveal: Technical analysis is not some mystical concept; it's a rigorous approach to investing that goes beyond gut feeling and media headlines. With a little help from history, patterns, and some well-placed lines on a chart, you can get a leg up on the market. Intrigued? Let's dig in.

What is Technical Analysis, Really?

Simply put, technical analysis is the study of market action, usually through price charts, to forecast future price movements. Forget earnings reports and economic indicators for a moment. Here, the price is king, and history has a funny way of repeating itself.

Price Charts: Your New Best Friend

The core of technical analysis revolves around price charts. Candlestick, line, bar—you name it. These aren't just squiggly lines on a screen; they're visual representations of human behavior. Every peak, every trough tells a story of greed, fear, hope, and regret. Learn to read this narrative, and you're well on your way to becoming a technical analyst.

Trends and Trendlines: Not as Boring as They Sound

Remember that old saying, "The trend is your friend"? It's the gospel truth in technical analysis. Markets tend to move in trends—upward, downward, and sideways. The trick is identifying these trends early enough to profit from them. How? Trendlines.

A simple line connecting the lows in an uptrend or the highs in a downtrend can act as a roadmap for future price action.

Moving Averages: Smoothing the Rough Edges
Price can be erratic, jumping around like a cat on a hot tin roof. Enter moving averages, the smoothing agents of technical analysis. Whether it's a simple moving average (SMA) or its more responsive cousin, the exponential moving average (EMA), these indicators can help you spot trends that aren't obvious in raw price action.

Resistance and Support: The Invisible Floors and Ceilings
In every market, there are levels where price seems to get stuck or reverse—like an invisible floor or ceiling. These are called support and resistance levels. Identifying these can give you valuable insights into entry and exit points. Think of them as the market's comfort zones, and you'll see why they're crucial.

Volume: The Fuel of Price Movement
Price doesn't move in a vacuum; it needs a catalyst. That catalyst is trading volume. Analyzing volume alongside price can give you a sense of the strength or weakness behind market moves. High volume during an uptrend? That's a bullish sign. But high volume during a downtrend? Watch out; the bears might be taking over.

Indicators and Oscillators: The Secret Sauce
Here's where it gets spicy. Beyond the basics, there are specialized tools like the Relative Strength Index (RSI), Moving Average Convergence Divergence (MACD), and Bollinger Bands. These are not random concoctions but mathematical formulas that help you fine-tune your analysis.

Is Technical Analysis Foolproof? Spoiler: No

Before you rush out to become the next market wizard, a reality check. Technical analysis is not infallible. It's a tool, not a crystal ball. Markets can, and often do, confound expectations. That's why risk management is crucial, but that's a topic for another day.

Why You Can't Afford to Ignore Technical Analysis

Even if you swear by fundamental analysis or consider yourself a passive investor, ignoring technical analysis is like driving with one eye closed. It equips you with the skills to navigate the market's ebbs and flows, offering an edge in an environment where every bit of information counts.

➔ To Sum Up: The Market's Not Random; It's Just Complex

Don't mistake complexity for randomness. The market may seem like a chaotic beast, but it operates on underlying patterns and behaviors that can be deciphered through technical analysis. Whether you're day trading or investing for the long haul, understanding these patterns is essential to your financial well-being. After all, if you don't take the time to understand the market's language, how can you expect to succeed in it? Technical analysis isn't just an option; it's a must-have skill in your investing toolbox.

9.2 Fundamental Analysis: The Sherlock Holmes of Investing

If you want to invest like the pros, you need to know more than just the stock price. You need to know the company inside and out. You need to be a detective, analyzing clues and piecing together a larger picture. That, in a nutshell, is what fundamental analysis is all about. Intrigued? Let's dive deep and decode the nitty-gritty of this powerful approach.

Unraveling the Mysteries of a Company

At its core, fundamental analysis is about dissecting a company to assess its true value. You look at everything from the financial statements to management's competency, from industry trends to the political climate. This is your toolbox for discerning whether a stock is underpriced or overvalued. Think of it as financial sleuthing, and the prize? A robust investment portfolio.

Financial Statements: The DNA of a Company

Think of a company's financial statements as its DNA, the coded instructions for how it operates. Here you find the balance sheet, income statement, and cash flow statement. These documents contain vital statistics about a company's health. Are revenues increasing? Is debt manageable? Does the company generate enough cash to fund its operations and growth? If you're not dissecting these statements, you're investing blind.

Ratios: The Cheat Codes of Analysis

Ratios like Price-to-Earnings (P/E), Debt-to-Equity, and Return on Investment (ROI) simplify complex financial data into easily digestible numbers. Each ratio provides a different lens to evaluate a company's performance and financial stability. P/E gives you an idea of what investors are willing to pay for a stock compared to its earnings. Debt-to-Equity provides insights into a company's leverage and financial risk. ROI tells you how effective the company is at generating returns. Ignore these at your peril.

Market Position: The King of the Hill Metric

How does the company stack up against its competitors? This is no trivial question. A dominant market position can act as a moat, protecting the company from economic downturns and competitive pressures. Look for brands that have stood the test of time, or disruptive newcomers carving a unique space in the market.

Management: The Hidden Variable

Great companies are often the result of stellar management. Who are the leaders steering the ship, and what's their track record? Are they aligned with shareholders' interests? Bad management can sink even the best business models, so don't underestimate this factor.

Macro Trends: The Invisible Hand

You could find the perfect company—excellent management, strong financials, and competitive advantage—but if it operates in a declining industry or a politically unstable region, all bets are off. Always analyze the bigger picture: technological trends, geopolitical stability, and the state of the economy. These macro factors often have a far-reaching impact on individual companies.

The Intrinsic Value: Your Personal Price Tag

Armed with all this data, the goal of fundamental analysis is to estimate the 'intrinsic value' of a stock. This is your personal price tag, the value you assign based on your comprehensive analysis. If the current stock price is below this intrinsic value, it's likely a good buy. If it's above, you might want to pass or sell.

Reality Check: It's Not Foolproof

No methodology is a guarantee against loss. Markets are influenced by a multitude of unpredictable factors, from sudden economic downturns to unforeseen company scandals. What fundamental analysis does offer is a robust framework for understanding the potential risks and rewards.

The Takeaway: Knowledge is Power

The more you know about a company, the less you have to rely on luck. Fundamental analysis allows you to invest based on facts and data rather than hunches and headlines. It equips you with the tools to make informed decisions, providing a solid foundation for long-term investing success. It's not just a technique; it's a philosophy that champions due diligence and informed decision-making.

So, if you're still relying solely on stock prices or tips from your neighbor, it's time to up your game. Start doing your homework, and become the Sherlock Holmes of investing. After all, in the world of investing, knowledge isn't just power—it's profit.

9.3 Behavioral Finance: Why Your Brain is Your Worst Enemy in Investing

When it comes to investing, your brain is not always your friend. In fact, it's often your worst enemy. Shocking? Perhaps. But behavioral finance—a field that blends psychology and economics—has mountains of research to prove it. If you've ever wondered why even the most logical individuals make irrational financial decisions, then sit tight, because we're about to dissect the quirks of the human mind that disrupt the rational flow of markets and investing.

The Irrational Human Element

Traditional financial theories, like the Efficient Market Hypothesis, assume that all investors are rational and have access to all available information. But let's get real. If that were true, bubbles, panics, and other market anomalies wouldn't exist. Behavioral finance acknowledges this irrational human element that can sometimes make the market look like a roller coaster driven by a toddler.

Cognitive Biases: The Usual Suspects

When we invest, cognitive biases cloud our judgment. These are hardwired shortcuts your brain takes to make quick decisions, and while they might have been useful for dodging saber-toothed tigers, they're disastrous for dodging poor investments. Here are a few notorious ones:

Overconfidence

Overconfidence leads people to think they're better at picking stocks than they actually are. The result? Excessive trading, high transaction costs, and ultimately, lower returns.

Confirmation Bias

People tend to seek out information that confirms their existing beliefs and ignore anything that challenges them. So if you're convinced a certain stock is a winner, you'll focus only on the positive news, conveniently overlooking any red flags.

Loss Aversion

The pain of a loss is psychologically twice as powerful as the pleasure of a gain. This is why investors often hold on to losing stocks too long, hoping they'll bounce back, while selling winning stocks too quickly to "lock in gains."

Herd Mentality: Follow the Leader to Your Peril

There's safety in numbers—or so our primitive brains tell us. Herd mentality explains why investors pile into the latest hot sector, driving prices up to unsustainable levels, and then scramble to get out, causing the bubble to burst. Following the herd may offer emotional comfort, but it's a one-way ticket to financial ruin.

Regret Aversion: The Paralysis by Analysis

No one likes regret. The fear of making a decision you'll later lament can be paralyzing. Investors suffering from regret aversion often stick to the status quo, missing out on opportunities because they're scared to make a move. Remember, doing nothing is also a decision—and often a costly one.

Emotional Rollercoaster: Greed and Fear

Two emotions dominate the investing world: greed and fear. Greed drives bubbles, while fear fuels panics. These emotional cycles are as old as markets themselves, and they create opportunities for those who can keep their heads cool while others are losing theirs.

The Solution: Know Thyself

You can't change human nature, but you can change your behavior. The first step is self-awareness. Recognize your biases and take steps to mitigate them. Use stop-loss orders to prevent emotional decision-making, diversify to minimize risk, and perhaps most importantly, consider seeking professional advice.

Financial Advisors: The Emotional Buffer

Even the most rational investors can benefit from an emotional buffer. Financial advisors provide that necessary barrier between you and impulsive decisions. A good advisor can help you stick to your investment strategy when emotions threaten to lead you astray.

Final Takeaway: You're Not as Rational as You Think

We all like to think of ourselves as logical creatures, especially when money is on the line. But the truth is, we're not. Our evolutionary instincts and emotional triggers interfere with rational financial decision-making every step of the way. Behavioral finance doesn't just expose these flaws; it offers a roadmap for navigating them.

➔ So the next time you're about to make an investment decision, take a step back. Are you being rational, or is your brain playing tricks on you? By understanding the psychological pitfalls that lie in wait, you can better arm yourself against your worst enemy in investing: yourself.

10. TAXES AND FINANCIAL INSTRUMENTS

10.1 Capital Gains and Losses: The Taxman Cometh for Your Profits and Losses

Taxes are a reality you can't avoid, especially when you're playing in the financial markets. You make a profit, the taxman wants a piece. You incur a loss, well, the taxman might offer some small comfort. This chapter isn't just a dull guide to tax compliance; it's your playbook to understanding, managing, and yes, even benefiting from the tax implications of your financial activities.

The Basics: What Are Capital Gains and Losses?
In layman's terms, a capital gain is what you get when you sell an asset for more than you paid for it. On the flip side, a capital loss is the financial hit you take when you sell an asset for less than your purchase price. Simple, right? But here's where it gets interesting. The tax treatment of these gains and losses is anything but straightforward.

The Timeline Matters: Short-Term vs Long-Term
You can't discuss capital gains and losses without mentioning the timeline. If you hold an asset for more than a year before selling, any profit you make is considered a long-term capital gain, taxed at a significantly lower rate than your ordinary income. If you sell within a year, that's a short-term gain, and it's taxed just like your salary. The message here is clear: for tax efficiency, patience is more than a virtue; it's a strategy.

How Much Will You Owe? The Rates
Here are the numbers you've been waiting for. As of my last update in September 2021, the long-term capital gains tax rates in

the United States ranged from 0% to 20%, depending on your income. Short-term gains? They're subject to your ordinary income tax rate, which can go as high as 37%. That's almost double the maximum long-term rate. See why timing matters?

Losses: The Silver Lining to Financial Missteps

If you incur a capital loss, all is not lost—in a tax sense, at least. You can offset your capital gains with your capital losses. Have more losses than gains? You can even use up to $3,000 of net capital losses to reduce your ordinary income. And if you still have losses left over, you can carry them forward to future tax years.

Wash Sales: The Taxman's Got Your Number

You might think you can sell a losing stock, claim the capital loss, and then buy it back immediately to maintain your position. Think again. The IRS prohibits this tactic through the Wash-Sale Rule. You need to wait at least 30 days before buying back the same or a "substantially identical" asset. Fail to do so, and you can't claim the loss.

Tax-Loss Harvesting: A Masterstroke or a Mirage?

Tax-loss harvesting sounds like a tactic reserved for the Wall Street elite, but it's accessible to everyday investors too. It involves strategically selling off losing investments to offset gains. But heed this warning: don't let the tax tail wag the investment dog. Make sure your decisions align with your overall investment strategy, not just your tax-saving goals.

When Do You Report Capital Gains and Losses?

You report your capital gains and losses when you file your annual tax return. That's when you'll get acquainted with forms like Schedule D and Form 8949. These aren't mere administrative hurdles; they're your tools for legally minimizing your tax burden.

Final Thoughts: Strategy Over Shortcuts

The tax implications of capital gains and losses aren't something you slap together at the last minute; they require strategy. Understanding the rules can help you make more informed decisions about when to sell or hold your assets. Taxes may be a certainty, but paying more than you have to is not. In the grand financial scheme of life, managing your capital gains and losses wisely could make the difference between an investment win and a financial fumble. So, learn the rules, consult with professionals, and remember: even the taxman offers opportunities for those savvy enough to seize them.

10.2 Dividends and Interest Income: The Subtle Art of Earning While You Sleep

Making money from your investments doesn't always mean buying low and selling high. No, there's another, often underappreciated way to profit, and that's through dividends and interest income. In this chapter, you'll learn how these payouts can be the silent engines driving your financial train forward—even when you're asleep.

What Are Dividends and Interest Income?
First, a quick refresher. Dividends are payouts you receive when you own shares in a company that decides to distribute some of its profits back to shareholders. On the other hand, interest income arises from debt instruments like bonds or savings accounts where you're essentially the lender.

Why Dividends Matter
Investing in dividend-paying stocks can offer a powerful combination of potential capital growth and regular income. But here's the kicker: historically, dividends have accounted for a substantial portion of the stock market's total return. It might not be as glamorous as skyrocketing stock prices, but dividend income is often more reliable, especially in turbulent markets.

The Tax Angle on Dividends
Tax-wise, dividends can be qualified or non-qualified. Qualified dividends are typically taxed at a lower rate than ordinary income—much like long-term capital gains. Why does this matter? Because understanding this can help you choose between holding

a dividend-paying stock and, say, a high-interest bond. Tax efficiency isn't just for the ultra-rich; it's a tool everyone should wield.

The Lowdown on Interest Income

Interest income from bonds or bank accounts is pretty straightforward. You lend money, and you receive interest in return. But be warned: this type of income is usually fully taxable as ordinary income, making it potentially less tax-efficient than qualified dividends. Also, in a low-interest-rate environment, the real return—after accounting for inflation—can be minuscule or even negative.

Tax-Exempt Interest: Not So Fast!

Sure, some bonds, like municipal bonds, offer tax-exempt interest. But remember, tax-free doesn't mean risk-free. Often, the lower yield on these bonds offsets the tax benefits. Plus, they're not universally tax-free; some could be subject to state or local taxes.

The DRIP Effect: Dividend Reinvestment Plans

Investors often overlook the power of reinvesting dividends through Dividend Reinvestment Plans (DRIPs). With DRIPs, you automatically purchase additional shares of the stock instead of receiving cash payouts. It's a set-it-and-forget-it strategy that lets the magic of compound interest go to work for you.

The Risks

Dividends aren't guaranteed. A company in financial distress can cut or eliminate its dividend at any time. Likewise, bonds can default. Always remember: there's no free lunch in investing. Balancing your portfolio to include both capital gains and income-producing assets can provide a safety net.

Timing Is Everything

In the investing world, specific dates determine your eligibility for dividends or bond interest. There are ex-dividend dates, record dates, and payment dates for dividends. For bonds, there are coupon payment schedules. Missing these deadlines can mean missing out on income you were counting on.

Reporting and Tax Forms: The Necessary Evil

For tax purposes, you'll often receive a Form 1099-DIV for dividends and a Form 1099-INT for interest income. These forms aren't just bureaucratic busywork; they're essential for accurate tax reporting. Don't underestimate them; penalties for incorrect reporting can be steep.

Final Thoughts

Dividends and interest income can be a lucrative part of your investment strategy if approached correctly. They offer not just potential income but also opportunities for tax planning and portfolio diversification. As the saying goes, it's not just about making money; it's about keeping it. By understanding the intricacies of dividends and interest income, you can do both. In a world obsessed with quick gains and high risks, the patient, informed approach to income investing can be a game-changer. It's time you leveraged these subtler, often overlooked aspects of investing to their fullest. After all, the best gains are the ones you can make while doing absolutely nothing.

11. ETHICAL CONSIDERATIONS

11.1 Socially Responsible Investing: Unveiling the True Power of Your Money

Your money has power. It's not just a medium for buying goods and services or accumulating wealth; it's an instrument for shaping the world. And that's where socially responsible investing (SRI) comes into play. This isn't some fluffy, feel-good concept; this is about aligning your financial goals with your moral compass. Buckle up; you're about to see investing in a whole new light.

What Is Socially Responsible Investing?
SRI is an investment strategy that considers both financial returns and ethical impact. You invest in companies that align with your social, environmental, and ethical values while avoiding those that don't. It's capitalism, but with a conscience.

The ESG Framework
At the core of SRI is the ESG framework—Environmental, Social, and Governance. Each of these categories has metrics that help investors evaluate a company's impact. Environmental criteria look at sustainability practices, social criteria examine human rights issues, and governance focuses on executive compensation and corporate transparency.

The Myth of Lower Returns
Many people hold a false belief that SRI equals lower financial returns. Let's debunk that myth right now: There's growing evidence that companies with strong ESG scores often outperform their less responsible peers in the long term. Good ethics can indeed make for good business.

Unpacking Impact Investing

Within SRI, there's a more aggressive approach called "impact investing." This involves proactively investing in ventures that produce measurable social or environmental benefits. It's not just about avoiding harm; it's about actively doing good. The impact is quantified, be it in gallons of clean water provided or tons of carbon emissions reduced.

The Various Flavors of SRI

SRI isn't a one-size-fits-all approach. There are various strategies, such as negative screening (excluding 'bad' companies), positive screening (selecting 'good' companies), and thematic investing (focusing on specific issues like renewable energy or gender diversity).

Your Values, Your Portfolio

One of the most empowering aspects of SRI is the customization. You don't have to accept pre-packaged "ethical" funds. Many investment platforms now allow you to tailor your portfolio according to your specific values. This means your money can be a direct extension of your beliefs.

The Risk Factor

Just like any investment strategy, SRI has risks. A company's ESG rating can change, or new information can come to light that contradicts its supposed ethical stance. Always do your due diligence.

The "Greenwashing" Dilemma

Be aware of "greenwashing," where companies exaggerate their ethical credentials. A pretty sustainability report isn't a guarantee of responsible behavior. Dig deeper and scrutinize third-party assessments to avoid this trap.

A Movement, Not a Trend

Socially responsible investing is gaining momentum, but it's not a passing fad. It's part of a broader societal shift toward conscientious capitalism. From institutional investors to millennials, people are waking up to the true power of money as a force for positive change.

The Global Ripple Effect

When you invest responsibly, you're not just making a statement; you're part of a collective effort that can shift entire industries. Large corporations are starting to feel the pressure from investors who demand ethical conduct, and this is influencing their policies globally.

The Regulatory Landscape

As SRI becomes mainstream, regulatory bodies are stepping in to provide frameworks and disclosure requirements. It's not just a wild west of good intentions anymore; it's becoming a structured, scrutinizable field.

➔ Wrapping Up

Forget the dated notion that finance and ethics operate in separate realms. Socially responsible investing proves that your investments can do double duty, earning you returns while making the world a better place. In this era of climate change, social inequality, and corporate misconduct, SRI isn't just a nice-to-have; it's a must-have. It's time to unleash the power of your portfolio for the greater good. Because let's face it: if your money could talk, what would you want it to say?

11.2 Insider Trading and Market Manipulation: The Dark Side of Finance Unmasked

Insider trading and market manipulation. It's the stuff of Wall Street dramas and SEC nightmares. But more importantly, it's the kind of behavior that shakes the very foundations of free and fair financial markets.

What Is Insider Trading?

At its core, insider trading involves buying or selling a stock based on material, non-public information. In simpler terms, it's cheating. Imagine sitting down for a poker game where one player can see everyone's cards. Not fair, right? That's essentially what insider trading does to the stock market.

The Legal Gray Areas

But hold on. Not all insider trading is illegal. Executives can still trade their own company's stock, provided they follow strict guidelines and reporting requirements. It's the unfair advantage gained from non-public information that lands people in hot water. Navigating this legal maze is no small feat, and many a career has been ruined for stepping out of bounds.

Market Manipulation: The Puppet Masters

If insider trading is about exploiting privileged information, market manipulation is about creating a false narrative. We're talking about tactics like "pump and dump," where a stock is artificially inflated to lure naive investors, only for the manipulators to sell, causing the stock to crash. Those who fall for the scam are left holding the bag.

The Costs Are Real

Let's be clear: Insider trading and market manipulation aren't victimless crimes. They corrode the integrity of financial markets and cost everyday investors billions. Your retirement savings? Your kids' college fund? All are at risk when these illicit activities go unchecked.

The Role of Regulation

So, who's in charge of keeping these financial rogues at bay? Enter the Securities and Exchange Commission (SEC) in the U.S., along with other international regulatory bodies. Their mandate is to level the playing field, and they have the power to issue crippling fines and even hand out prison sentences.

High-Profile Cases: The Who's Who of Scandal

From Wall Street titans like Ivan Boesky and Raj Rajaratnam to homemaking icon Martha Stewart, the list of those caught in the insider trading web is long and diverse. These high-profile cases serve as cautionary tales, but they're just the tip of the iceberg. For every big fish that gets caught, there are countless minnows that slip through the cracks.

Whistleblowers: The Unsung Heroes

In this shadowy world, whistleblowers are the unsung heroes. These brave individuals often risk their careers to shed light on corrupt practices. Recent laws have made it more lucrative and secure to be a whistleblower, but the emotional and professional toll can be immense.

Technology

Advancements in technology have been a game-changer in detecting illegal activity. Sophisticated algorithms can now flag unusual trading patterns in real time. However, the same tech also aids those looking to skirt the law, creating an endless cat-and-mouse game between regulators and rule-breakers.

Ethical Implications: Beyond the Legalities

Lastly, let's talk about the elephant in the room: ethics. The legality of insider trading and market manipulation is one thing, but the ethical bankruptcy involved is another. Even if one escapes the clutches of the law, the moral stain remains. And for what? Short-term gains at the expense of long-term trust and integrity.

➔ It's time we stopped romanticizing the rogue traders and market manipulators as cunning mavericks. They're not. They're undermining the very system that allows for wealth creation and economic growth. As investors and participants in this ecosystem, it's our collective responsibility to be vigilant, to educate ourselves, and to support the structures that aim to preserve the sanctity of our financial markets. Because if we don't, we're tacitly allowing the erosion of one of the cornerstones of modern capitalism: a free, fair, and transparent marketplace.

12. ADVANCED TOPICS

12.1 Algorithmic and High-Frequency Trading: The New Titans of Wall Street

The world of trading has undergone a seismic shift, and if you're still romanticizing the idea of a Wall Street filled with human traders shouting orders across a chaotic trading floor, wake up. The new titans of Wall Street are algorithms and high-frequency traders, and they've turned the market into their high-speed playground.

What is Algorithmic Trading?
Algorithmic trading uses mathematical models and computer programs to execute trading orders automatically, based on a variety of market factors. We're talking about machines making split-second decisions about buying and selling, decisions that a human simply cannot make as rapidly or precisely. The focus is efficiency and maximizing profits through superior speed and intellect—albeit artificial intellect.

And High-Frequency Trading?
High-Frequency Trading (HFT) is a subset of algorithmic trading but dialed up to eleven. These algorithms execute trades in milliseconds or even microseconds. They scan the markets for tiny price discrepancies and act before you've even blinked. The trade sizes might be small, but when you're making thousands of them per second, it adds up.

The Role of Technology
This is an arena where the best tech wins. Custom-built computers, high-speed data feeds, and co-location services (where the trading computers are kept as close to the exchange

computers as possible) are the new tools of the trade. It's a far cry from the notepads and shouting of yesteryears.

How They Change the Game

Both algorithmic and high-frequency trading impact the market in ways traditional trading never could. They offer unprecedented liquidity, making it easier for other traders to find counterparties. But they can also cause rapid and irrational market fluctuations. Remember the "Flash Crash" of 2010? That was a wake-up call to the risks posed by these high-speed trading methods.

Ethical Questions

Ah, yes, let's not gloss over this. Is it fair? Is it ethical for a computer program to outwit a human trader simply because it can process information faster? These are heated debates, often split down generational lines. While it's hard to say if these methods are unethical, they certainly challenge our traditional understanding of a level playing field.

Regulation: Playing Catch-Up

Regulators like the SEC are perpetually playing catch-up with the fast-paced changes in trading technology. They've introduced measures like "circuit breakers" to halt trading if an asset's price moves too rapidly, but it's akin to putting a Band-Aid on a bullet wound. The speed and complexity of these trading methods often outstrip the regulators' understanding.

Social Impact: Widening the Gap

The rise of algorithmic and high-frequency trading also widens the gap between the haves and the have-nots. Big trading firms can spend millions on the best algorithms and the fastest computers, leaving retail investors and smaller firms in the dust.

It's capitalism at its most ruthless, where money and technology create an impenetrable moat.

The Future: AI and Beyond

And we're not done. The future holds the promise—or threat, depending on your view—of trading algorithms powered by artificial intelligence. These would be self-learning systems, capable of adapting their trading strategies in real time. It sounds like science fiction, but it's closer than you think.

➔ Conclusion: Adapt or Perish

Here's the harsh reality: the game has changed, and it won't revert to the old ways. Algorithmic and high-frequency trading are here to stay, and they will continue to evolve. Your choice is to adapt or be left behind. Understand how these systems work, the opportunities they offer, and the risks they pose. Because if you're not at the table, you're on the menu. So, stop romanticizing the "Wolf of Wall Street" era. Those days are over. Today's market is a high-tech arena, where algorithms rule and speed is king. And whether we like it or not, this is the new face of trading and the new titan of Wall Street.

12.2 Dark Pools and Private Exchanges: The Shadowy Corners of Finance

Let's rip the Band-Aid off: the financial market you think you know—the one with transparent transactions and regulated exchanges—is just the tip of the iceberg. Beneath that surface lies a murky, less-visible world of dark pools and private exchanges. This isn't some James Bond intrigue; it's a practical reality that impacts the market, whether you like it or not.

What Are Dark Pools?

Dark pools are private financial exchanges where the details of the trades are concealed until they are completed. They're like invite-only parties where institutional investors trade large blocks of shares without tipping off the entire market. Why does this matter? Because if you're selling a massive amount of stock, doing it in the open market would be like yelling "fire" in a crowded theater—you'd cause a panic and drive the price down.

And What About Private Exchanges?

Private exchanges are similar but differ in one crucial aspect—they're more customized, tailored to the specific needs of participants. Think of it as a VIP room within the already exclusive club. These exchanges cater to unique asset classes or specialized trading needs that mainstream exchanges can't handle.

So, Are They Legal?

Here's the catch: yes, they're legal, but they operate in a regulatory gray area. They're subject to less oversight compared to public markets, which is a double-edged sword. It allows for flexibility but also opens the door to potential abuses, such as price manipulation and information asymmetry.

The Appeal: Why Do They Exist?

The appeal is straightforward—dark pools offer anonymity, reduced market impact, and cost savings. Institutional investors love them for these reasons. But let's be clear: these benefits primarily serve the big players in the market, not the average Joe.

Why You Should Care

You might think, "I'm not an institutional investor; why should I care?" Well, you should. Dark pools and private exchanges can influence the prices and liquidity of assets on public markets. When large trades happen in the shadows, they can create information imbalances that affect retail investors in the public markets.

The Ethical Quagmire

It's time to talk about the elephant in the room: ethics. These platforms were initially created to serve legitimate needs, but their secretive nature raises ethical questions. The primary concern is that they perpetuate inequality between institutional and retail investors. The big guys get a more efficient, cost-effective trading venue, while the small investors are left to navigate the choppier waters of public markets.

Regulation: A Cat-and-Mouse Game

Regulators are on it, but it's like playing whack-a-mole. Every time a rule is implemented to increase transparency or fairness, new tactics emerge to skirt around it. The Securities and Exchange Commission (SEC) and Financial Industry Regulatory Authority (FINRA) have started to impose stricter reporting requirements, but enforcement remains a challenge.

Future Prospects: A Balancing Act

Looking forward, the future of dark pools and private exchanges hinges on finding a balance between flexibility and transparency. Blockchain technology, for instance, is being considered for its potential to provide anonymity while ensuring transaction integrity. But make no mistake—the landscape is shifting, and how it changes will affect everyone, not just the elites.

➔ **The Takeaway: Ignorance Isn't Bliss**

Listen, it's easy to overlook what you can't see, but ignorance isn't bliss in the world of finance. Dark pools and private exchanges are integral parts of the modern financial landscape. If you choose to ignore them, you do so at your own peril. So educate yourself, be aware of the impacts, and be prepared for how these shadowy corners of finance might affect your investments. In the end, dark pools and private exchanges are not going away. They serve a purpose, but they also serve a select group of participants at the potential expense of the broader market. Whether you view them as a necessary evil or a beneficial innovation, the fact remains: they are a potent force in finance that you can't afford to ignore.

**If you liked this book,
please leave a good review on Amazon.**

Don't forget to check out our guides and courses on www.exafin.net